Rethinking
Recess

Rethinking Recess

Creating Safe and Inclusive Playtime for All Children in School

REBECCA A. LONDON

HARVARD EDUCATION PRESS
Cambridge, Massachusetts

Copyright © 2019 by the President and Fellows of Harvard College

All rights reserved. No part of this publication may be reproduced or transmitted in any form or by any means, electronic or mechanical, including photocopy, recording, or any information storage and retrieval systems, without permission in writing from the publisher.

Paperback ISBN 978-1-68253-414-4
Library Edition ISBN 978-1-68253-415-1
Library of Congress Cataloging-in-Publication data is on file.

Published by Harvard Education Press,
an imprint of the Harvard Education Publishing Group

Harvard Education Press
8 Story Street
Cambridge, MA 02138

Cover Design: Endpaper Studio
Cover Photo: FatCamera/E+/Getty Images

The typefaces used in this book are Lunaquete Corsa Grotesk, and Miller.

To my daughters,
Jessica and Zoe

And to children everywhere,
who deserve the right to play

CONTENTS

Introduction: The Case for Recess   1

PART I
Understanding Recess Today

1. Current Inequities in Recess   15
2. A Snapshot of Recess Across the Country   35

PART II
Improving Recess for All Children

3. Organizing and Customizing Recess   61
4. Building a Culture of Play at Recess   81
5. Social and Emotional Learning Thrives at Recess   105

PART III
Supporting Recess Through Policy and Practice

6. Local Policies and Practices to Support Recess   133
7. Improving State and Federal Recess Policies   153
8. The Right to Play   171

APPENDIX 1: Resources for Rethinking Recess 185
APPENDIX 2: Great Recess Framework–Observational Tool (GRF-OT) 187

Notes 193
Acknowledgments 205
About the Author 207
Index 209

INTRODUCTION

The Case for Recess

On a sunny April weekday in California, fourth- and fifth-grade students at Northside Elementary School eagerly walked with their teachers from their classrooms to the school's outdoor yard.[1] Northside is a school that serves mainly Latinx students, more than half of whom entered school as English learners, and the majority of whom receive free and reduced-priced meals. Students could barely keep still with excitement for their impending recess time. They gathered outside for a brief moment to learn about the games that were set up by Coach Diana, a paraprofessional who was hired by the school specifically to support recess. She directed students' attention to the day's options: soccer on the field to the left, three-line basketball or knockout on the courts, and four-square on the four-square courts. Jump ropes were laid out by the basketball court, and Coach Diana advised students not to jump too close to the basketball game. She also invited students to play dodgeball with her and made a few other suggestions, including walking and talking and practicing gymnastics on the grass, which she had noticed was a new activity that the fifth-grade girls enjoyed. She left them with a final reminder that there is no running on the blacktop and that everyone should be following school rules in all the games. With that, Coach Diana blew her whistle, and the students chose where they wanted to start their recess period.

Coach Diana selected the games and activities carefully that day, building on her work throughout the school year to organize the outdoor space into predictable places where certain kinds of activities take place. She intentionally designed recess to help students establish common rules to games that everyone could agree on and to reflect what students in fourth and fifth grade most like to play. She created options for them where they could feel safe—physically, emotionally—to have fun, take risks, and be part of an inclusive school environment. If only every school had a Coach Diana.

If only every school had recess.

Rethinking Recess: Creating Safe and Inclusive Playtime for All Children in School draws on a decade of field research, policy analysis, and exploration of the literature, to make the case for rethinking how schools provide recess. In addition, this book was written to offer specific guidance for school leaders, policy makers, community organizers, and others interested in actionable approaches for supporting equitable, high-quality school environments.

In this book, I focus not only on day-to-day recess practices, staffing, and funding considerations but also on larger state and federal policy contexts that affect recess time.

Recess is an essential part of the elementary school experience. Too often, though, recess is an afterthought—a blank space in the middle of the packed school day. I believe, and research supports, that there should be an intentionality around recess design where recess plans are developed like classroom plans, with attention to safety, health, social and emotional learning, and engagement.

Simply offering recess is insufficient to elicit students' engagement in safe and healthy play. The book introduces a purposeful approach to organizing recess and presents key tools to enhance its effectiveness as a learning space, including conflict resolution, inclusivity, and student leadership. The book also tackles policy considerations, including the use of recess withholding as punishment and how state and federal policy can better promote high-quality recess. With planning and support, recess can meet students' social, emotional, and physical developmental needs and create an environment in which students feel safe and can have fun.

The Right to Play

The word *recess* means a brief interlude for relaxation between periods of work, or in other words, a break. These breaks are not unique to students and schools. Adults take breaks during their days too—lunch breaks and courtroom recesses, to name two. Breaks are not a luxury. Research shows that taking breaks increases the productivity of adult workers because the time away from work reenergizes them to focus better when they return.[2] Evidence also points to the detrimental effects of sitting in one place for long periods of time; medical professionals now recommend that adults who are seated for their jobs take a break and move around every thirty minutes.[3] Growing in popularity, the latest time management strategies even suggest using a timer to separate bursts of work time with short breaks.[4] Historically, the vast majority of US elementary schools also had built into their daily schedules one or two short breaks for recess. Beginning in the late 1980s, the assumption that recess is a necessity changed.

Elementary schools at that time began to reduce or even eliminate breaks for children during the school day. There's a cultural and historical context for this unfortunate and, in my opinion, damaging and costly shift. In the late 1980s, international student performance comparisons demonstrated the underperformance of US students relative to their peers in other countries, spurring a desire for domestic reforms aimed at closing that gap. This reform effort culminated with the No Child Left Behind Act in 2001, which put into place a standards-based accountability framework that required schools, school districts, and states to meet certain benchmarks or risk sanctions, including loss of funding and, worse, the reconstitution of the school under new management. Student performance was measured by standardized tests in two subjects: math and English language arts. This focus on standardized testing led to enormous pressure for administrators and teachers, particularly in schools that were underperforming on these tests, to improve math and English test scores. This pressure, in turn, led to prioritization of instruction in these two subjects over so-called nonessential subjects. Recess was among the periods during the day that was reduced or eliminated in favor of more instructional time in core subjects. Along with art and music, recess became expendable.

Counter to the notion that students, like adults, need a break to improve their productivity and well-being, many school districts—notably Atlanta, Baltimore, and Chicago—took the drastic step of eliminating recess altogether, even for very young children in elementary schools. Estimates suggest that in the five years after No Child Left Behind was first implemented, 20 percent of elementary school districts had shrunk their recess time, averaging a reduction of fifty minutes per week.[5]

Still, recess had its supporters. During this time, major human rights, policy, and advocacy groups began to offer position statements on the importance of play for children and recess in schools. In 1989, nearly every nation worldwide signed the United Nations Convention on the Rights of the Child, which states, "That every child has the right to rest and leisure, to engage in play and recreational activities appropriate to the age of the child..."[6] Educational organizations—including the National Association of Early Childhood Specialists, National Association for the Education of Young Children, Association for Childhood Education International, National Association of Elementary School Principals, and National Association of State Boards of Education—followed with position statements and reports that demonstrated their strong support for recess time in elementary schools.

At the same time, a public health crisis was gripping the nation. Between 1988 and 2007, the obesity rate for elementary-aged children increased by 75 percent, with one-fifth of children in this age group categorized as obese in 2007.[7] Since that time, obesity rates have leveled off and even declined slightly, but this dramatic rise prompted responses from public health agencies to implore schools to use recess as a way to increase children's physical activity during the day. Public health advocates have indeed been successful; the focus of recess policy since that time has been on increasing minutes of physical activity available to children. States have even begun to mandate minutes of daily recess, all in an effort to increase children's opportunities for exercise. This effort is an important start, but it is not enough. This single-minded focus on physical health overlooks the challenges schools face with their recess time—including disciplinary referrals, exclusion, and bullying—and does not recognize the other important benefits recess can support.

On this front, the tide is again turning. Two powerful public health organizations have weighed in on the importance of recess, and significantly, both have included in their statements an acknowledgment that supporting an emotionally and physically safe recess requires school planning and staff training. In 2013, the American Academy of Pediatrics issued a policy statement that identifies both the value of recess for elementary students as well as key features of what it considers to be a well-run recess.[8] This was the first time that the organization acknowledged that attention to what happens at recess is an important part of making sure recess is meeting students' developmental needs. In 2017, the Centers for Disease Control and Prevention along with SHAPE America released two reports that detail strategies for improving elementary school recess.[9] The guidance they offer embraces recess as a place where social and emotional learning is solidified, in addition to an opportunity for exercise in the school day.

The Importance of Recess

How recess is supported and what happens during that time is critical if students are to reap its benefits. Many adults have an idyllic view of recess from their own childhoods, thinking of it as a carefree break from an unrelenting school day filled with rules and behavioral expectations. Even today, many elementary students will tell you that recess is indeed their favorite subject. For others, recess can be a stressful and even scary time. Despite research that points to the multiple benefits of recess, it can be unsatisfying or even detrimental to students if children are unprepared to initiate and sustain their own games, if adults act punitively rather than supportively, if conflicts and bullying occur unchecked, and if the recess culture promotes winning over engagement as the ultimate goal of play. Rather than address these challenges, many schools have neglected or overlooked recess as an important part of students' school day.

It is well documented that young children learn and develop in valuable ways through play. Those who advocate for school recess time have organized themselves into camps espousing two different types of play: free play with minimal adult interference and structured play, which is more like a physical education class. I contend that this is a false dichotomy. Those who champion free play reason that without adult interference, children use their imaginations to drive their play and that they learn important lessons about how to navigate complex social issues. While this outcome might be true for some students in some schools, in many schools, unregulated recess time without purposeful adult guidance ends with students lined up outside the principal's office to be admonished for their poor behavior. In schools that do not pay attention to recess, it can be a chaotic and disorganized time, which can be stressful for both children and adult supervisors. These kinds of recess periods are likely not able to promote the developmental growth that recess has the potential to help students accrue. On the other end of the spectrum is a structured recess, which offers adult-led games and activities without free choice and is more like a physical education class. This kind of rigid approach to recess might result in more minutes of exercise or pedometer steps, but it restricts opportunities for children to grow socially and emotionally through negotiations that happen in more unstructured play.

In this book, I introduce the concept of an "organized recess," which is a hybrid between free play and structured recess times. Organized recess is achieved through thoughtful programming and staff training and promotes a recess time that is safe, healthy, and fun; it offers opportunities for enhancing students' social and emotional development. It provides more order than a free play recess by making clear the game offerings and game rules, but also embeds free choice and opportunities for imaginative play. In organized recess, multiple games with common rules are present, students know conflict resolution strategies, students have free choice and games are inclusive to all who want to play, and adults support students through prosocial modeling. Research demonstrates the efficacy of this approach on a variety of outcomes, including improving school climate and decreasing bullying.[10] Important life lessons are hard to learn when recess is not operating at its full potential, but with intentional scaffolding, all children can benefit from this valuable time and learn through play.

What are these benefits of recess? The health benefits are unmistakable: recess affords students opportunities for physical activity, which is important to meet the American Academy of Pediatrics' recommendation of sixty minutes per day of activity.[11] More than just a way to address obesity, exercise is important because it helps children to concentrate, improves their self-esteem, and has even been associated with reduced depression.[12] Physical activity has been associated with improved cognition in children and adults.[13] There is also evidence of a strong link between physical activity during the school day and students' academic performance.[14]

Other benefits of recess are equally as important, including improvements in student classroom behavior.[15] Having a well-designed recess in place reduces the amount of time classroom teachers spend helping their students resolve post-recess problems; one estimate shows teachers can gain as much as the equivalent of a full day's instruction simply from improving recess.[16] In addition, during a well-designed recess, elementary students engage in a variety of play activities that can help them learn and practice skills such as conflict resolution, decision-making, compromise, and self-regulation. When students have productive recess time, they can use it to build relationships with peers and adults, especially those whom they may not see in their classrooms. Relationship building is especially important because recess experiences affect both students' and teachers' perceptions of school climate.[17] Finally, recess is a key time in the school day that can support students' development socially and emotionally.[18] For elementary school students, social and emotional skill development helps them to manage their emotions, show respect and empathy for others, and create positive relationships with peers, among other outcomes.[19] Rather than detract from students' learning, research has shown that promoting social and emotional learning at school is strongly associated with improvements in academic achievement across grade levels.[20]

Educational reforms today include deliberate efforts to promote positive school climate. A positive school climate reflects a school's attention to fostering students' and adults' feelings of physical and emotional safety, strong student-adult and student-student relationships, and student and adult connectedness or engagement to school, as well as creating a supportive academic, disciplinary, and physical environment.[21] As with social and emotional learning, efforts to enhance school climate are associated with improved academic and mental health outcomes for students.[22]

Reforms to enhance school climate and social and emotional learning often overlook recess as a prime opportunity for reinforcing their goals. Yet, the evidence offers strong justification that recess is a vital context for these reforms to take root. I firmly believe that a well-designed and purposeful recess can help children to accrue developmental gains and have fun, while still benefiting the school goal of academic learning. When recess is designed to be safe and healthy, it serves the students' developmental needs, improves the school climate, reduces disciplinary issues, and reclaims precious minutes of instruction time in the classroom.

The State of Recess Today?

Here is the good news: As a result of multipronged advocacy efforts and the realization on the part of administrators that eliminating recess may not be what is best for students after all, we are currently seeing a resurgence of recess. Responding to concerns about students' needs for both more physical activity and mental break time, eight states, from Colorado to Connecticut, have enacted policy changes that would ensure children's right to recess every day.[23] Although a comprehensive source of information on how many schools offer students recess and for how long is not yet available, evidence suggests recess is on the rise. Atlanta, Baltimore, and Chicago—those large school districts that abolished recess—have now reinstated it. Between 2000 and 2014, the share of elementary schools that reported providing regularly scheduled recess for their students increased from 71 percent to 94 percent.[24] Yet, the most recent estimates indicate that only 20 percent of school districts nationwide have policies *mandating* daily elementary school recess, and 60 percent have no official recess policy at all.[25]

Although data suggest that recess is on the rise, when considered from an equity lens, the issue of recess provision takes on a new level of urgency. Students who are from underrepresented minority or lower socioeconomic status backgrounds are more likely to be enrolled in schools that do not offer regular recess.[26] Removing recess denies these children key learning opportunities and midday breaks that we know help to solidify classroom learning.

Even where daily recess is included in the bell schedule, substantial groups of students may miss out because recess time is withheld for misbehavior, unfinished school work, or other issues. There is little research on the frequency and effect of withholding recess, but available evidence suggests that policies allowing recess to be withheld for behavioral issues or to complete school work are significantly more prevalent at schools with higher concentrations of low-income students.[27] For teachers, withholding recess, which is many students' favorite time of the school day, is perhaps the most salient threat they can make to keep students behaving in class. Yet, the notion of withholding recess from students who have trouble behaving or concentrating in class is counterintuitive because it is precisely these children who need a break to get their wiggles out or refocus their brains. The repeated removal of certain students from recess for punishment sends signals to these students that they do not belong and are incapable of being socialized with their peers, and is among the very first steps in the school-to-prison pipeline.

Today, when recess is having its resurgence, we have a new opportunity to ensure equitable access to play, physical activity, and social and emotional development for *all* elementary schoolchildren. Offering recess every day to every child is an important first step, but simply offering recess is not a guarantee that it will be a productive time for students. This book recognizes the renewed interest in using recess time productively and provides a springboard for using research-based strategies to design high-quality recess plans for all schools to engage students, improve school climate, promote healthy lifestyles, and support academic learning as well as social and emotional development.

About the Research

In 2009, I was first introduced to leaders at Playworks, the only national nonprofit organization of which I am aware that is actively engaged with educators to reframe recess as a critical time for positive development among students and support their safe and healthy play throughout the school day. This initial conversation led to a decade of collaboration to understand what recess reform looks like, the necessary inputs for lasting change, and the ways that recess reform can benefit children and adults in school. This research, funded by the Robert Wood Johnson Foundation, serves as the basis for this book. The examples and lessons learned are drawn from three major studies that my colleagues and I conducted in partnership with Playworks. In total, this research includes thirty schools implementing programs associated with Playworks and twelve schools that were randomly assigned (as part of one of the studies) to a control group that was interested in reforming recess but delayed formal implementation for one year during the study.

In the first project, we set out to understand the experiences of six newly implementing schools and two established schools as they went about reforming their recess times in Northern California. Using extensive field notes and rich description, we were able to characterize the transition of the play yard throughout the school year. The second study was a national randomized controlled trial that assessed the impact of the program on a variety of student outcomes in five regions. My colleagues at Mathematica Policy Research were responsible for the quantitative or impact portion of this study, and my team of researchers were on the ground assessing recess operations and student engagement at recess in both the treatment and control schools. In an effort to expand access to safe and healthy recess across the country, Playworks began to shift its work toward empowering schools to improve their own recesses through providing ongoing training to their own recess staff. The third study included six regions nationally and focused on how school leaders make changes to recess that align with their existing school policies and programs.

In each of these studies, data collection included interviews with principals, teachers, recess coaches and aides, and in some cases Playworks national and regional staff; observations of multiple recess periods at each school spanning all elementary grades; and focus groups with fourth- and fifth-grade recess leaders. Research teams participating in these studies included doctoral students and master's-level staff researchers, both men and women, representing a diversity of ethnic backgrounds. I also rely on annual surveys of staff and administrators at hundreds of schools nationally and a survey of elementary principals collected by the Robert Wood Johnson Foundation and Gallup in 2010.

These rich data, spanning from 2005–06 to 2015–16, cover diverse geographic locations and student populations, representing a variety of school contexts, recess and school policies, recess yard setups (including one on an urban rooftop!), and other factors that affect student and staff recess experiences. Schools served predominantly low-income populations and were located mainly in urban school districts nationally. The anecdotes shared in this book come directly from this research. Names of individuals, schools, and regions have been changed to protect the identities of the research respondents, who were assured confidentiality when they agreed to participate in the studies.

The lessons from Playworks and other research in this book point the way for the future. Improving recess requires that educators, administrators, and policy makers understand the difficult situations present every day on the play yard and then implement a diverse array of solutions so that all children can have the recess they need to grow and learn. *Rethinking Recess* is intended to help them. As such, the book is organized into three parts that help readers to understand and overcome the challenges of recess time. The first part focuses on recess today and why a renewed focus on recess time is essential. Chapter 1 explores how the accountability movement and other current recess policies have created deep inequities in who has access to the benefits of recess to make the case for focusing on improving recess policy and practice. In chapter 2 I build on this case by going inside schools and drawing on a large survey of principals to illustrate why recess in the United States—of wildly variable quality and a common source of unnecessary discipline referrals—is in need of reform. The second part offers specifics on how to improve recess environments at the school site, including a focus on engagement, as well as social and emotional learning. In chapter 3, I expand on the tenets of an organized recess and break down the steps recess advocates can take to plan a better recess. Chapter 4 goes into more detail on how to create a culture of play at recess by embedding inclusivity, student leadership, and conflict resolution. Chapter 5 reports on the social and emotional progress for students that ensues when schools attend to recess in the ways described. Part 3 of the book explores the role of educational leadership and policy makers in supporting purposeful recess for all children. Chapter 6 considers local policies and practices that can support improved recess environments, and chapter 7 focuses on state and federal policy. Chapter 8 concludes with an analysis and synthesis of the findings and offers guidance for the future of policy and educational leadership moving toward a more effective recess for all children.

Today, we understand that recess is not a disposable period in the school day, but instead it's a time that contributes strongly to students' academic learning, social and emotional growth, and physical development. Unfortunately, this period with limitless potential has been eliminated in many schools. And worse, recess has been jettisoned inequitably, serving to further marginalize students who face the most barriers to academic success.

In this book, I propose we bring recess back to every elementary school and use this opportunity to rethink recess not only for the students who have been without recess but for all elementary school students. With intent, planning, and commitment on the part of educators and policy makers, recess can live up to its potential of providing students with a break from their structured classroom that supports their whole child development. More than ever before, today's generation of learners must be academically prepared and also savvy in skills such as collaboration, negotiation, self-control, and empathy. Where can they learn and practice these essential twenty-first century skills? At recess!

PART I

Understanding Recess Today

CHAPTER ONE

Current Inequities in Recess

In 1998, at the height of the standards-based accountability movement, Benjamin O. Canada, then superintendent of Atlanta Public Schools, famously commented to the *New York Times*, "We are intent on improving academic performance. You don't do that by having kids hanging on the monkey bars."[1] Atlanta was one of the first public school districts to eliminate recess altogether, with district administrators making the case that students can get their physical activity in physical education class, so any midday breaks for recess are simply taking away from instruction in core content.[2] It was not the only school district to take this approach; up to 40 percent of schools eliminated recess, cut back on recess, or were considering one of these options according to a 1999 survey of more than fifteen thousand school districts.[3] It wasn't until the mid-2000s that Atlanta schools reversed course and again offered breaks to elementary students, but by then the damage had been done. Schools had been built without playgrounds, students and teachers were unfamiliar with recess routines, and any school culture that supported regular and productive recess had been lost. How did this happen? In Atlanta as well as many other school districts nationwide, recess was assumed by well-meaning but ill-informed administrators to be outside of the academic realm. With increasing pressure to show improvements in math and English, recess was cut in favor of "butts in seats" academic preparation. Today we know that this is flawed thinking, but the vestiges of these decisions from two or more decades ago remain in many schools.

Why is this flawed thinking? Experts in the fields of education, pediatrics, and child development agree that providing recess to elementary children aids their academic growth and is therefore an important and necessary part of the elementary school day; simply put, children who have breaks learn better. One reason for this is that recess provides an opportunity for physical activity, which stimulates cognition and helps students to focus and pay attention. In addition, having an unstructured break allows children the chance to practice key social skills and develop emotional regulation strategies through their interactions with peers and adults, both of which aid in classroom learning. A productive recess contributes to a positive school climate for both students and teachers, and decades' worth of research has shown that a positive school climate associates with higher academic performance.[4] Conversely, time spent in recess does not detract from student learning; there is no demonstrated relationship between spending less time in recess and gains in student educational outcomes.[5] In short, recess is not a break from learning; it is in fact a critical component of learning.

To understand the state of recess today—and why it should be a focus for school leaders and reforms—it's important to begin this book with a look at the large role that recent education policy has played in not only minimizing attention to the type of learning that serves students' developmental needs but also in determining who has the opportunity to access this type of learning. The standards-based accountability movement created a natural experiment that tested the elimination of recess in elementary schools. But the experiment was not random in its selection of schools for cutting and keeping recess. In districts and schools that underperformed on standardized tests, administrators were more likely to cut recess in favor of more time for academic instruction. Schools serving underrepresented minority students as well as those with high concentrations of low-income or English learning students comprise many of these so-called underperforming schools. Take Atlanta, for example. When Atlanta Superintendent Canada made his comments about how to promote academic achievement by dropping recess in schools, 89 percent of students in that urban school district were African American.[6] As statistics in the next section will show, in schools that were already meeting the levels required by standards-based accountability—schools that served higher income, suburban, white children—recess was preserved at higher rates.

I discuss multiple equity issues embedded in recess in this chapter. First, because the elimination of recess that happened through the standards-based accountability movement did not happen randomly, schools that served underrepresented minority, low-income, and urban students were the most likely to experience cuts in recess. In other words, there is inequality in access to recess, which further marginalizes already vulnerable students by withholding an important setting for developing life skills and embracing physical activity that will help children to succeed in school and beyond. If children are not getting these experiences in other nonschool settings, due to neighborhood safety concerns or lack of access to sports leagues, recess is an even more important period for schools to embrace. Second, although not all schools have reduced or eliminated recess, even in these schools, inequities are present. For instance, recess may be withheld from certain students as punishment for disciplinary problems in the classroom. We know that African American boys and students in special education are the most likely elementary students to experience school discipline, so policies such as withholding recess may negatively impact these groups more than others. Finally, underfunded schools, particularly urban ones, may lack the space or equipment to support a productive recess for students. In some locales, schools built during the standards-based accountability era did not include an outdoor play space, making the reinstatement of recess challenging. To tackle a problem, we must first acknowledge and understand it. This chapter lays out areas of inequity in our current recess landscape and makes the case that attention to equity in recess is important so that all children have the opportunity to learn through play at school.

The Recess Opportunity Gap

In 1991, Chicago Public Schools, like Atlanta beforehand, eliminated recess entirely from the school day. At that time, the urban Chicago schools served mainly African American (57 percent) and Latinx (28 percent) children;[7] almost the same percentage (84 percent) received free and reduced-priced meals in the 1990s, a proxy that educators and educational researchers use for indicating low-income status.[8] National statistics demonstrate that the elimination of recess from underrepresented minority and low-income students is more than just a localized policy. A study published in the journal *Pediatrics* used data on third-grade students from a nationally representative sample in 2001 and found exactly the same pattern.[9] Descriptive findings from this study are shown in figure 1.1. Among white third graders, 23 percent were in schools with no or only minimal recess. For Latinx children, the percent with no or minimal recess jumped to 38 percent, and for African American children, 59 percent had no or minimal recess. This problem is concentrated almost entirely among public schools because very few children in private schools had their recess restricted. Low-income students (40 percent) and those in large or middle-sized cities (37 percent) were much more likely to have recess eliminated or drastically reduced compared to higher-income students (20 percent) or those in large or middle-sized towns (30 percent) or in small towns or rural areas (19 percent).[10]

FIGURE 1.1   Percentage of third-grade students with access to school recess

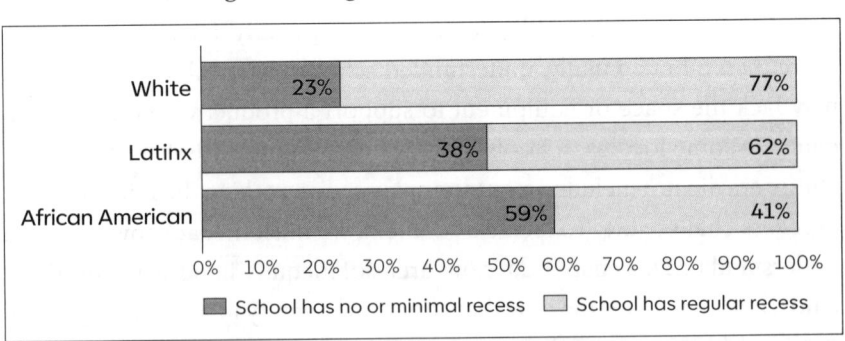

Source: Barros, Romina M., Ellen J. Silver, and Ruth EK Stein, "School Recess and Group Classroom Behavior," *Pediatrics* 123, no. 2 (2009): 431–436.

These statistics mirror other documented inequities embedded in our educational system. The "opportunity gap" in education refers to the disparities in access to high-quality school experiences, including instruction, facilities, and other supports available for lower-income or underrepresented minority students compared to wealthier white students. Much of the research on the opportunity gap focuses on access to high-quality instruction and challenging course material, but these data on recess access point to a more fundamental problem. When the opportunity gap reaches into students' time for play and physical activity, society denies only a certain segment of the population an opportunity to develop as a whole child at school—academically as well as socially, emotionally, and physically. What are the reverberating effects of this? We do not know, but denying only lower-income or underrepresented minority children the opportunities to develop through play is extremely troubling.

The Recess Data Gap

With many other statistics—including teacher quality, instructional minutes, test scores, school discipline incidents, and even attendance—data collections are available to support documentation of the opportunity gap. With recess, however, data are inadequate to even understand the problem, much less track it annually to document changes. The School Health Policies and Practices Study, conducted by the Centers for Disease Control and Prevention, is the best source of information available on school-level practices regarding recess in elementary schools. However, the survey is conducted every other year, and the content varies between survey administrations. In some years it includes detailed information such as minutes offered, plans for inclement weather, timing, and practices for recess discipline, but in other years only a subset of these measures is tracked. School-level data, as opposed to data on students' experiences, also do not account for variations in individual teacher or yard monitor recess practices, which can vary even within a school. In other words, even if a school regularly offers recess, certain students may have their recess time revoked repeatedly, and school-level data do not allow for tracking the experiences of students to see which are the most affected.

Other data also offer periodic glimpses into recess inequalities. Several studies rely on the Early Childhood Longitudinal Survey, which follows students starting in the early 2000s and asks about individual student experiences with recess. However, the data are not collected annually for new groups of elementary students. Some surveys collect information from students or principals periodically but not consistently over time. The compilation of information available about recess provision and access is therefore insufficient to fully characterize the extent of recess inequality present today or to allow us to follow any changes in inequality over time that may have resulted from changes in policy at the state and local levels. Being able to consistently document the problem and to track the effectiveness of changes in policy or practice is an important part of any policy debate, and in the case of recess, our data collection efforts are woefully behind.

Obstacles to Play Outside the School Day

Observers have posed a number of arguments in favor of reducing play time in schools to allow more instructional minutes, chief among them that children can get their play time at home. However, research points to obstacles to active play outside the school day for precisely the children whose recess time is most in jeopardy due to factors such as neighborhood safety and access to play environments or sports leagues.

In her extensive research on recreation spaces in Chicago, Monika Stodolska and her colleagues demonstrate the complications that urban children and youth face in finding safe outdoor space for recreation. Their research shows the problem of gangs and crime in thwarting neighborhood recreation; gangs have infiltrated many urban parks in Chicago, and these parks can serve as spaces for drug use and distribution.[11] Even if the park itself is free of crime, access to parks can require crossing through rival gang territory, which makes outdoor spaces similarly inaccessible. Indeed, a study that focused on youth strategies for navigating outdoor recreation showed that fear of crime limited youth participation in physical activity when they were at home in their neighborhoods.[12]

A second constraint to children's play opportunities at home is access to outdoor space. In many communities, there are not even opportunities to access recreational spaces outside of school because these spaces simply do not exist. Research focused on the built environment—including green spaces, public pools, bike paths, and other recreational spaces that promote physical activity—shows a tremendous inequality in access to outdoor spaces.[13] Communities with lower overall socioeconomic status and those where underrepresented minority families congregate not surprisingly have the least access to spaces that enable outdoor physical recreation. Another study found that although all neighborhoods tend to have recreational facilities one can pay to use, ironically low-income neighborhoods have fewer free facilities to use for physical activity.[14]

One place that young children often learn about games and sports, as well as get physical activity, is through organized extracurricular sports leagues. In many urban areas, a multitude of opportunities flow out of city Parks and Recreation departments, police or sheriff athletic/activity leagues, and private sports leagues such as youth soccer and Little League baseball. Unfortunately, there are no reliable estimates of how many elementary-aged students participate in these organized sports; even the US Report Card on Physical Activity for Children and Youth focuses exclusively on high school students in its analysis of extracurricular sports participation.[15] In my own research, principals and teachers across the country have reported that their students do not participate in these leagues very often, either because the leagues or the equipment needed are costly and families are not able to afford them, or because they require children to be at practices and games at certain times of day and parents cannot get them there. Costs of sports programs vary depending on the sport and level of play. Competitive sports leagues can require outlays of thousands of dollars, even at the elementary school level, once costs associated with professional coaches, travel, and uniforms are factored in. Little League baseball and other local recreational youth sports leagues, such as soccer and basketball, cost less, and programs put on by a city agency or the local YMCA might be offered on a sliding pay scale so that they are free to the lowest-income children. However, these programs still require children to have properly fitting equipment and footwear, which must be replaced as children grow. They also require that children be present at practices and games—often just one or two hours at a time—and parents who work multiple jobs, have odd hours, or have unreliable transportation may not be able to get their children to and from these activities at the appropriate times. Many principals and teachers in my research have lamented that because of these constraints, their students come unprepared to play at recess, which results in the problems they frequently encounter—conflict, disciplinary incidents, bullying, boredom, unsafe play, and exclusion. Rarely have they connected this underpreparation to a need that the school can fill through its own attention to recess.

Perhaps societal considerations affect out-of-school activities and play time? The education sociologist Annette Lareau wrote about children's extracurricular activities in her award-winning book *Unequal Childhoods*.[16] Through a detailed exploration of family life for lower- and higher-socioeconomic status families who are both white and African American, she concludes that some differences in parenting follow socioeconomic status lines. The higher-socioeconomic status parents embrace a strategy she calls "concerted cultivation," in which they intentionally select activities for their children (often too many) that help them to develop their skills in specific ways. In contrast, the lower-socioeconomic status parents follow a strategy she calls "natural growth," where they promote more family interaction with cousins and other extended family as playmates and fewer, if any, organized extracurricular activities. This explanation for why certain children participate in extracurricular activities has been criticized, pointing out, as I have seen in my own research, that income and time constraints are often barriers that families find difficult to overcome when it comes to their young children participating in organized sports.[17] This debate highlights the complex relationship between family culture and access to particular kinds of recreation, including play and physical activity outside of school.

As a whole, this body of work suggests that the combination of safety, family values, access, and constraints all come to bear in whether and how much children are playing games and sports outside of their school contexts. The research literature calls into serious question the notion that urban children from lower-socioeconomic status families and under-resourced communities are able to have their play and physical activity needs met outside of school.

Play as an Aid to Social and Emotional Learning

The research on inequality in access to recreation points to an obvious solution: children can get these health- and development-promoting activities at school. However, as I've now made clear, priorities in the field of education shifted away from providing play opportunities during the school day. The decisions to eliminate or shorten recess have reverberating consequences, and these consequences disadvantage already marginalized students. Without recess, students lose an opportunity to accrue time toward the sixty minutes of physical activity per day that is recommended by the American Academy of Pediatrics. Particularly for the students whose neighborhood opportunities for physical activity are constrained the most, those who are low income or living in urban areas, fewer minutes of recess are offered at school.[18] The reason for some of this may be that schools built in the post-recess era were built without playgrounds. Again, no universal data exist on the facilities available at elementary schools nationwide, but estimates indicate that in Chicago, which had eliminated recess for several decades, nearly one hundred elementary and middle schools were built with no playgrounds at all.[19]

In addition, denying access to recess limits students' opportunities to learn and grow through play. Play is how children learn some of their most fundamental lessons. Anthony Pellegrini is a University of Minnesota psychologist who is one of the most notable researcher-advocates for children's play and school recess; in his many publications he stresses the importance of peer-to-peer interactions among young children as essential for their social and emotional development. He writes, "[C]hildren learn and practice the skills necessary to interact in the larger social world from their peers. They do this, not through direct tuition, but through ordinary give and take with their peers."[20] He goes on to note that the role of play is essential in social and emotional development because it involves formal and informal rules that children must integrate through their interactions with peers. Learning to take turns, follow rules, and compromise for the sake of the larger goal of interacting with peers requires a variety of behaviors that children need time to practice. Pellegrini argues that this practice is important not only for their social and emotional development, but also for their cognitive functioning in the classroom. It's not simply that recess and play offer a break from learning that can help children get out their wiggles; the development that happens through play and interaction with peers is part of the learning process.

At Northside Elementary in California, where Coach Diana had organized the play yard in an attempt to help more students become engaged in play, Mr. Ramirez, the school's principal, told us that the play yard was not always this well-run. In an interview during the fall of that school year, he lamented the changes that standards-based accountability brought to his low-income school and talked about what his students need at recess.

> *And with more and more focus in the classroom being on testing and academics and stuff, I hate to say it, but teachers have really cut back on the amount of time and energy they want to focus on teaching kids PE, especially when you're talking five-, six-, seven-year-olds. So, as a result, what we find is that, and whether this has something to do with our particular community, because of the economic situation, most of our parents . . . our parents are not typically the ones who have their kids in softball or in a professional, some sort of service outside that teaches them. So, a lot of the kids who come in, they don't know how to play games. So, that was the frustrating thing, was that even something as simple as you give a group of kids a soccer ball and you assume they're just going to get together and form a team and put a goal, no, it just becomes a ball that they chase after and inevitably get into fights.*

Principal Ramirez stated what my research team heard from many administrators and teachers across the United States—that play outside of school is no longer where children learn important skills about conflict resolution and self-regulation, how to start a game and keep it going, and how to play for the fun of playing and not only to win. It's not necessarily that they don't have the physical skills needed to play a particular game—although sometimes this is the case—but rather that they do not have the social and emotional experience to create a sustainable game on their own and enjoy playing whether they win or lose. If children are not learning these important life lessons out of school, and their recess time in school is shortened or eliminated due to academic or disciplinary concerns, then as a society we are experiencing a crisis of child development.

Not only children lose out when recess is reduced or eliminated. In the first recess study I conducted, my team and I documented a strong link between changes in recess culture in the schools we visited and overall perceptions of school climate for students and teachers.[21] Our research demonstrated the ways that intentional improvements in recess culture over the course of one school year could benefit the overall school climate because students were happier and more satisfied after recess, they had forged relationships with peers and adults on the recess yard, they were less likely to bring their recess-time problems (if any) into their classrooms, they had learned simple conflict resolution skills, and they had been encouraged (with moderate success) to use positive rather than negative language in their play interactions. We found through both qualitative and quantitative data that as the recess climate goes, so does the overall school climate. In addition, improvements in overall school climate are associated with improved academic and mental health outcomes for students.[22] Our research focused on schools with existing recess periods that were looking to make improvements, but a logical extension of this work would posit that adding a well-planned and productive recess time in schools without recess periods could add tremendously to school climate.

Psychologist Pellegrini has been a strong advocate for recess and has weighed in on controversial decisions like the one in Atlanta to eliminate recess. Although he has not couched his support for recess in an equity lens, his research corroborates the argument that denying recess to children creates inequities in access to developmental settings that support their positive growth and learning. Policies that allow removing recess for certain children or allow the wholesale reduction or elimination of recess for certain segments of the population of schoolchildren based on demographic characteristics or test scores create inequalities in social and emotional learning that can have lasting effects.

Discipline and Withholding Recess

Even where daily recess is included in the school bell schedule, substantial groups of students may miss out because recess time is withheld for misbehavior, unfinished schoolwork, or other issues. As is the case with recess denial overall, evidence suggests that there may be inequalities in which students are withheld from recess. Regardless, keeping students out of recess for punishment or missed schoolwork is antithetical to the goals of academic learning.

Estimates vary by data source, but somewhere between half and three-quarters of elementary schools nationwide allow teachers or monitors to withhold recess from students at their discretion. Data from the Centers for Disease Control and Prevention's 2014 School Health Policies and Practices Survey indicate that 45 percent of elementary schools do not have policies that prohibit or discourage staff from excluding students from all or part of recess as punishment for bad behavior or failure to complete class work.[23] A survey of almost two thousand elementary schools nationally shows slightly different results. In 2011, 72 percent of schools surveyed allowed teachers to withhold recess for poor student behavior, and 76 percent allowed withholding recess for missing schoolwork.[24] In about a third of these schools, these practices were discouraged but still allowed. This same study also found that schools with more students on free and reduced-price meals, a proxy for low socioeconomic status, had more restrictive recess policies, but no differences were based on student ethnicity. Probably the most important finding from this research is that policies matter. Schools in districts with strong policies that prohibit withholding recess are much less likely to allow teachers to withhold recess from individual students for punishment or to make up schoolwork.

This information is some of the best we currently have regarding policies for withholding recess in elementary school, yet there is still much we do not know. We have little sense of how often these policies are put into practice, and for how many and which students, including whether certain types of students are disproportionately punished through recess withholding. No research exists on what happens to children who are affected by recess withholding, including how this makes them feel and whether withholding recess is in fact a deterrent for future misbehavior. Although a substantial body of literature discusses children's play at recess, the experiences of children who are not allowed to play at recess are not documented because these students are often kept indoors or sent to a detention room, beyond the purview of researchers who observe what happens during recess. It is important to learn more about the students who are kept out of recess and how this treatment affects their schooling experiences. In elementary school students begin to form their schooling identities and see how they fit into society. Being told repeatedly that they do not belong in the only time set aside for socialization in the school day could negatively affect students' self-perceptions and their sense of belonging at school.

A study of student experiences with discipline in twenty Oregon elementary schools sheds some light on the issue. Using data from an online disciplinary referral database combined with other school records and surveys, researchers found that in these twenty schools, 55 percent of disciplinary incidents resulted in a time-out, particularly spending recess or part of recess "benched." The next two most common consequences were the removal of a privilege, such as being banned from the play structure at recess, or being held inside from recess altogether.[25] These modes of punishment entail withholding privileges or experiences from students, presumably those they care about most, but when children are punished by withholding play repeatedly, they miss important opportunities to learn about and practice meeting behavioral expectations, and schools lose opportunities to teach children about these expectations. These early disciplinary actions enforced by elementary schools can have lasting effects on students, as these can be their first punishment experiences in the well-documented school-to-prison pipeline, which has been demonstrated to begin as early as elementary school.[26] If children learn early on that their behavior warrants special treatment—withholding privileges and removal from group activities—but are not provided environments and opportunities that support them to change that behavior, schools and teachers have missed an important opportunity for intervention.

Two major issues with conflict and disciplinary actions at elementary schools must be explored to fully appreciate the potential for recess inequity even when recess exists. The first is that recess is the place where many disciplinary referrals originate in elementary schools. A study of automated office referral data in over one thousand elementary schools showed that almost one-fifth of all office referrals for disciplinary problems stem directly from the playground.[27] The primary location for referrals is the classroom, which makes sense because elementary students spend the vast majority of their school day within their classroom, but the most common timing of these classroom disciplinary referrals is the noon and 1 p.m. hours. This is just after lunch and recess, suggesting that not all conflicts or disciplinary problems are resolved where they originate, and even if students are not disciplined at recess, their recess problems may carry over into their classrooms.

A second major issue is that disciplinary referrals and subsequent consequences are more common for certain students, namely boys, African American children, and children with disabilities. The comprehensive US Department of Education's Civil Rights Data Collection shows clearly that African American students in K–12 are the most likely to experience disciplinary actions at school and that these actions occur in disproportionately high levels relative to their representation in the population.[28] This is especially so for elementary students, although special education students are also disproportionately disciplined in elementary school.[29] It has been suggested that special education students are punished for behaviors that result from their diagnoses (e.g., autism), and it is worth noting that the same children who are disproportionately overrepresented in school discipline are also overrepresented in special education, namely African American and English language learner children.[30] The combination of using recess withdrawal as a punishment and the disproportionate disciplinary enforcement of students from certain demographics is a key equity issue. Withholding recess isn't good for any children, but withholding recess from certain demographics of children in much higher rates than others is evidence of inequality.

After a year of intensive work on the play yard by Coach Diana and students at Northside Elementary, in an interview at the end of the school year, Principal Ramirez noted the remarkable changes that happened not only with play but also with school discipline as a result of intentionally changing the recess culture:

> *What I was hoping for... was an increase in a lot of activity by kids and a decrease in number of fights. We still have kids who get into trouble, but they're more outliers; they're the kids who—I hate saying this—but there are some kids who are just... they're going to look for it.... But what was happening in the previous years is that those kids who would have their own agenda, and a whole group of kids who were bored and had nothing else to do, who were otherwise not troubled kids, would follow them. Whereas, this year, those kids are much more isolated. And we still... I'm not saying we don't have any suspensions or any activities like that, but I don't remember the last time we had a serious fight of kids actually going at each other and hitting each other. Whereas, last year, [in] the last few months of the year, we dealt with quite a bit of that. Whereas, this year... we've had suspensions, but they've been for things like just outright disrespect or things that have not really been... we haven't had any suspensions for big, all-out, you know, "We're going to jump on some kids and beat him up." That hasn't happened.*

It may be surprising to hear Principal Ramirez talk about elementary students jumping and beating each other up, but this is the reality for elementary school principals in many urban areas today. Principal Ramirez could have chosen to abolish recess to keep students at Northside Elementary safe, as many others have done. Instead, he chose to rebuild his school's recess to make it a safer environment for all students. As Anthony Pellegrini says, "It is true that kids get bullied on playgrounds, but they get bullied in cafeterias, too, and in hallways, in bathrooms, in locker rooms, just about anywhere with little or no adult supervision."[31] Eliminating or withholding recess will not solve disciplinary problems at schools. Rather, taking away a key time in the school day when children can learn important skills like conflict resolution creates problems by not allowing students a chance to learn. However, having proper supervision and a plan for engaging students is a necessity for recess to reach its potential. I argue throughout this book that when recess time is planned in the same way as classroom time, all children will have an opportunity to engage in safe and healthy play.

Play Yard Space and Weather

At Northside Elementary, as with many other schools nationwide, changing the recess culture has been key to disrupting school disciplinary problems. At Northside, some of this change had to do with reestablishing trusting relationships with students. The school's outdoor yard is *L*-shaped, and with a limited number of recess safety monitors, a certain area of the play yard had been closed because it was not easily visible. Closing this part of the play yard was a problem because this area had the painted markings on the ground for common playground games like four-square that students wanted to play. Without access to that area, students' game and space options were limited. As Coach Diana worked with students at recess, she began to introduce games back into the closed area. Students were thrilled to have four-square and other games reintroduced. Through careful attention to game rules and expectations, as well as a change in how the space was monitored for safety, the closed portion of the *L* was reopened with an understanding that if students misbehaved, it would be again closed. But students did not misbehave and it remained open all year. The administration showed they were willing to trust students, and the students responded to that trust by meeting expectations.

Still, Northside students were fortunate to have a large play area for students to access. Even with part of the *L* closed, the play area had enough space to safely support multiple grades at recess at once in a variety of games. This is not always the case at elementary schools, particularly in central cities. Geographically, there are gross inequalities in the spaces students can access at recess. Data from the more than thirty schools my research teams have visited in the past decade demonstrate that regional differences matter tremendously. Nearly every school we visited was part of an urban school district, but schools in the urban West Coast, Pacific Northwest, and Mountain regions, for instance, tend to have substantially more space and especially green space than schools in the major metropolitan areas of the

East Coast. In these areas especially, urban schools with limited outdoor space and neighborhood safety concerns may have a more difficult time providing daily recess for all students than schools in suburban or rural areas that do not face these challenges.

The state of recess depends heavily on the outdoor play space available and the fixed and nonfixed equipment available. Fixed equipment like play structures or permanent goal posts can create natural boundaries for types of play, which can be an asset but can also be a problem if the space is small and the fixed equipment limits the types of games or activities that can be played. For instance, a large play structure in a small yard limits running games like soccer or tag and creative games that children initiate themselves. A dominant play structure promotes certain kinds of play that revolve around existing equipment (e.g., swinging on monkey bars or climbing on "rock" walls). As play specialists will argue, this kind of equipment limits children's learning and development because it is more structured and offers fewer opportunities for creativity. On the other hand, fixed equipment can also create safe spaces for children who have a hard time joining in with larger games and activities. If the equipment is old and not in great shape, then the fixed equipment may be less appealing to students while still limiting the other kinds of activities that can take place in a small area.

Weather is another key factor that adds to regional inequality in access to outside spaces for play. Necessarily, when the weather is very cold, very hot, or rainy, alternative plans for indoor recess must be made. In some regions, these cold or rainy conditions last for months, whereas in milder climates children can be outdoors throughout the school year. Colder climate schools often have better indoor facilities than warmer climate ones, including gymnasiums and auditoriums, that can be used to create play spaces during cold weather. When high temperatures or rain make it unsafe for children to be outside in warmer climate schools, their indoor alternatives are often limited because these schools were built without gynmasiums or auditoriums, or these spaces (mainly auditoriums) double as cafeterias. At one school I visited, the sign on the door of a multiuse space read "Cafetorium," indicating its primary use as a cafeteria that can be turned into an auditorium if needed. In this school, located in a mild but rainy climate, this space was not available for play activities on rainy days.

The Importance of Reviving Recess for All

The spaces that schools occupy and their environmental contexts can create inequalities, but this book is not about how to gain more space or change the weather. It's about how to combine the resources available with supportive school policies to create a positive recess environment for all students.

Attention to recess is essential for creating positive developmental spaces during school breaks, and doing so equitably requires new provisions that are currently not in place in most states. Provisions are in place to ensure equity when it comes to some aspects of schooling, however, including the recent move toward the Common Core State Standards to align nationwide standards by grade. State policies that prescribe certain numbers of instructional or physical education minutes are another way of ensuring equitable inputs to education. With recess, which I argue is fundamental to learning and social and emotional development, few provisions are in place to ensure equitable access across and within schools. Without this attention to what happens at recess, equity in access to developmental growth and learning opportunities will not be achieved.

Since the fateful decision to abolish recess in favor of more time for reading and math, Atlanta's recess story has taken a new direction. In 2005, Atlanta Public Schools reinstated a suggested fifteen-minute unstructured break on days when physical education was not offered to students.[32] Without using the word *recess* or offering an admission of faulty policy or a strong endorsement of the value of recess for students, this policy change opened the door for school administrators to begin to offer breaks for students during the school day. During the next school year, a group of organizations that included the Cartoon Network, National PTA, and Centers for Disease Control and Prevention (which is in Atlanta) collaborated to champion recess at National Recess Week.

In 2017, the Atlanta Board of Education again made strides toward more equitable recess access by approving a student- and parent-supported measure to forbid teachers from withholding recess as a punishment for disciplinary issues.[33] This measure is among the most important ways that school administrators can ensure equity in recess provision and at the same time help their students to gain important physical, social, and emotional developmental growth, which are all important for continuing academic progress. In 2018, the Georgia legislature took the recess debate to a new level, with the House approving legislation to mandate thirty minutes of recess per day for Georgia schoolchildren. However, the Senate approved a weaker version, which the House also then approved, but the legislative session ended and the governor did not sign or veto the bill.[34] The legislation is back on the docket in 2019.

Policy changes are necessary first steps for changes in practice but are often insufficient to ensure on-the-ground transformation. In places where recess has been abolished and reinstated, institutional knowledge about how to engage students in meaningful play at recess has been lost. In all schools regardless of recess history, inattention to creating productive recess time can result in breaks that are unsatisfying to students, or worse, damaging to the learning process. Recess should be planned just as class time is, with thoughtful consideration of its developmental goals and how to achieve these goals for students in different age groups. Among this book's aims is to provide the tools, strategies, and research that will support administrators, teachers, parents, coaches, and policy makers who must do the work of rebuilding recess, equitably, in all elementary schools.

CHAPTER TWO

A Snapshot of Recess Across the Country

Barbara Johnson had been the principal of Lafayette Elementary School, an inner-city neighborhood school, for almost a decade. She has seen the neighborhood change as higher-income families moved into the traditionally low-income community because of its affordable housing. Now, the school demographics also are starting to change with this shift, but some of the worst neighborhood conditions still existed for her students, as she described:

> The neighborhood is ... there are less and less people allowing their children out into the streets. We have a, south of our school, the houses are restored row houses and they're going for, you know, $250,000, $280,00 for a row house. And [north of the school], there's some that are in great shape and they may sell for $125,000, $140,000. But there's also a lot of just abandoned buildings. It is a high drug trafficking area. It's a high murder rate. It has not been unusual for us to have a murder going on, have occurred in the neighborhood over the weekend, and we have both the victim's family and the

> *defendant's family in our building, which really makes for a dicey situation. For example, we just . . . this weekend, the seventeen-year-old that was murdered . . . is the older brother of one of my students. So, you just deal with it.*

In this school and many others, students face enormous hurdles to succeed due to the entrenched and complex societal issues that produce the high crime neighborhoods in which they live. For these young students, school could be their safe haven. On the day we visited to observe recess at this school, field notes indicate that it was not. One class of students in a mixed-age lower-grade recess was kept indoors for punishment during their one recess break at lunch. It's important to note that this was a prearranged observation day, as we traveled to get there, so Principal Johnson knew we were coming and what we would be doing during our visit. We do not know why these students were denied recess but presume, based on context, that the lunch monitors did not like their lunchtime behavior. This kind of recess withholding is a fairly common occurrence and is often the result of the misbehavior of a few students or that the class is behind on its daily work.

The older students at Ms. Johnson's school did have recess on the day we visited, but their recess was not a safe haven from the neighborhood problems either. The field notes describe what recess for third through fifth graders was like on this day:

> *There was a very negative vibe to this whole recess. Although there was a fair amount of physical activity in spurts, it was all to run away from being punched or tackled. There were a lot of students not at the recess at all because of schoolwork or punishments, and it seemed like an unpleasant experience for those who were there. The actual time that students were out on the yard was quite short—only about ten minutes total—but that time was full of bullying and negative play. An overall concern here is how many students are having recess taken away from them as a punishment.*

In addition, the field notes describe adult monitors not interacting with children, no games set up, and children standing idly or alone.

Unfortunately, on this day and on many other days at different schools across the country, a short recess filled with conflict and chaos is not atypical. This recess did not support the many growth opportunities that a recess period can provide, and this example stands in contrast to what we heard from Principal Johnson, who told us in her interview that she understood that recess was a time for children to grow socially and emotionally and she was hoping to make changes to promote these outcomes. The experiences of students at Lafayette Elementary are not isolated examples of recess gone wrong. Recess withholding is quite common, and unfortunately, in the schools I have visited, a negative recess environment is also not unusual. Principal Johnson acknowledged that her school's recess time was not living up to its potential and was looking for help from programs like Playworks to create safe, healthy, and productive recess spaces for their students.

In this chapter, I weave together findings from two sources of original data to tell a story about the state of recess today and why it is in need of rethinking. The first is data collected as part of a randomized controlled trial of the recess reform program Playworks. I focus on the twelve schools that were selected to be part of the control group that was not included in the program that year but offered the intervention in a future year. My team—composed of myself, a doctoral student, and several master's-level researchers together representing a variety of ethnicities and genders—visited these twelve schools that were all interested in improving recess conditions but not necessarily taking steps to do that. All schools had at least 50 percent of students qualified for free and reduced-price meals and were located in five urban and geographically diverse areas. I concentrate on these schools to explore what recess looks like in schools that acknowledge they need recess reform but haven't started it. In later chapters, I focus on the schools that were working with Playworks to improve their recess.

The second data source is a 2010 survey, conducted by Gallup and the Robert Wood Johnson Foundation (RWJF), of nearly two thousand elementary principals nationwide to better understand their recess needs and experiences.[1] Gallup and RWJF generously granted my request to reanalyze these data for this book so that I can offer more details about how principals view recess, especially contrasting the experiences of schools that serve different populations of students. I combine information from this survey with my own observations and interviews at twelve schools nationwide to paint a picture of what recess is like for elementary students today.

Disparities in Access to Recess

All the principals who responded to the Gallup/RWJF survey indicated that their school had daily recess scheduled for all students. This response is unsurprising because principals who do not have recess scheduled for their students would probably not respond to a voluntary survey about recess!

How much recess they offered varied tremendously depending on their location and the students they served.[2] As is shown in figure 2.1, among both urban low-income and all other schools, the vast majority held recess every day (89 percent in urban low-income schools and 94 percent in all other schools).[3] However, disparities existed in the amount of recess students received. In urban low-income schools, students were far more likely to have a half an hour or less of recess than in all other schools. It's unclear

FIGURE 2.1 Extent of recess in urban low-income and all other schools, days per week and minutes per day

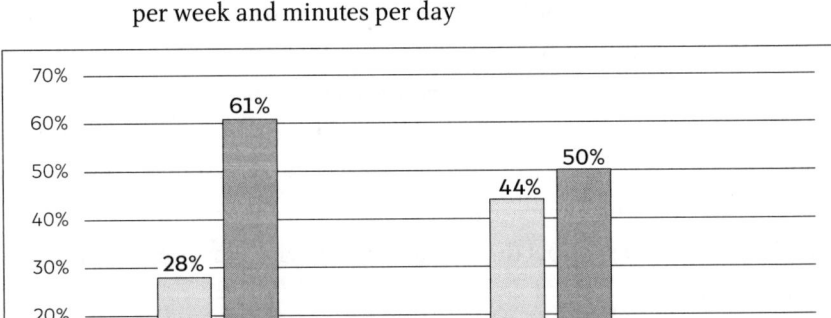

Source: Gallup/RWJF survey of principals

from the survey whether the minutes also include time children spend eating lunch. In most schools, students have about a half-hour break midday during which they eat lunch and have time for recess, so even though some schools reported a total of thirty minutes, students may actually have gotten fewer than fifteen minutes to play once they ate lunch and moved between the lunch and play areas.

State and local policy played a role for some principals in their recess scheduling. One-third of principals reported recess was required by a local or state governing body; slightly more than half reported that it was not. Seventeen percent of principals did not know if a local or state recess policy existed that covered their school. Some principals also acknowledged that pressures related to student achievement and their progress toward annual goals set by the US Department of Education influenced the amount of recess in their schools. Although many principals noted this pressure, it was particularly an issue for principals in urban low-income schools. In these schools, concerns about meeting student achievement goals led to decreases in recess time for 28 percent of principals, compared to 19 percent in all other schools.

Variations in Student Engagement at Recess

Principal respondents to the Gallup/RWJF survey were clearly fans of recess; the majority of principals surveyed believed that recess has a positive impact on academic achievement and students' abilities to listen and stay focused in class, as well as on their social development and general well-being.[4] This belief aligns with how Principal Johnson felt about recess as well, even though what we observed on the day of our visit was far from an ideal recess environment.

When asked about their students' engagement at recess, principals responding to the Gallup/RWJF survey reported a remarkable, and perhaps overly enthusiastic, sense of recess engagement (see figure 2.2). More than 90 percent of principals reported their students engaged in team play/sharing at recess frequently or constantly, and 95 percent reported their students getting physical exercise. Nearly all principals reported students were socializing with the same sex, but fewer reported they were socializing

FIGURE 2.2 Student activities during recess, as reported by principals

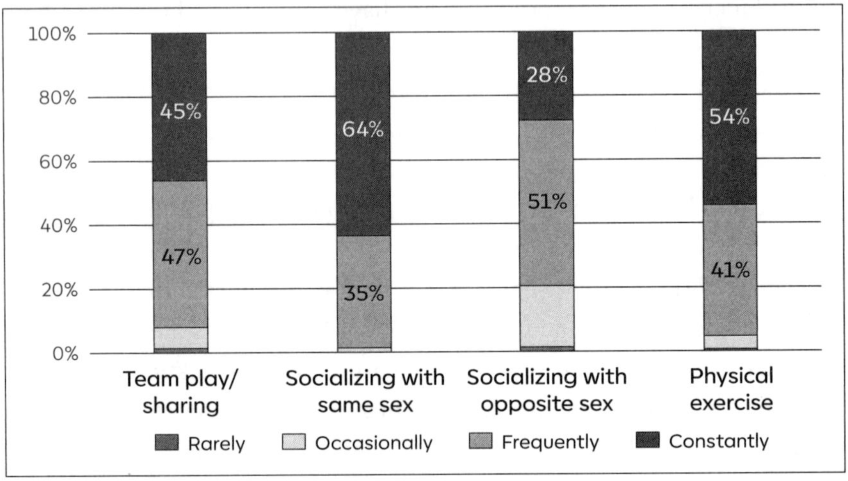

[Stacked bar chart showing percentages for Team play/sharing: 47% Occasionally, 45% Constantly; Socializing with same sex: 35% Occasionally, 64% Constantly; Socializing with opposite sex: 51% Frequently, 28% Constantly; Physical exercise: 41% Occasionally, 54% Constantly. Legend: Rarely, Occasionally, Frequently, Constantly.]

Source: Gallup/RWJF survey of principals

with the opposite sex. The question asks, "Please indicate how often each of the following behaviors occurs during an average recess period..." and goes on to request information about team play/sharing, socializing with members of the same or opposite sex, and physical exercise. These are not mutually exclusive categories, of course, because you can be playing and getting exercise, or socializing and playing, or playing with boys and girls together.

What these statistics miss is some nuance. Take, for instance, team play/sharing, which nearly all principals agreed is something their students do routinely. Does that mean students are engaged in team play or sharing the entire recess period? Are all students engaged in that way, or are there variations by gender and age? Is that play sustained throughout recess, or does it exist in short spurts and end in conflict? Are there reasons why some students might not be engaged in team play/sharing during recess, such as inadequate equipment or space, bullying, or exclusion? My team's recess observations help to explain what's behind these numbers.

At one school in a fourth- and fifth-grade recess, boys were playing a basketball game. This play would count, in the survey, as both team play and physical exercise, as well as possibly socializing with the same sex. However, the field notes from that recess reveal a problem:

> *At first, the basketball game seemed like a good example of positive play with boys cooperating and playing together. Then an argument derailed the game entirely, and they were unable to get the game moving. Worse, they continued to argue as they left the court and moved into line and also while they were waiting in line [to go back inside].*

This description of students being unable to move beyond a disagreement to keep playing and then going back to class still feeling unresolved is a common story that we heard not only with competitive games and older boys but also with all kinds of activities, ages, and genders.

We also observed recesses where students technically were getting physical exercise, but we would not characterize the activities as a positive recess environment. In another school, which had more limited equipment and space, an observer of a kindergarten and first-grade recess made this note in field notes:

> *This recess has very little structure to it and, while kids are running quite a bit, very few are playing any games beyond what might be a massive game of tag. The space itself is not very conducive to playing games because the lines are too faded to use and the grass isn't really a field appropriate for playing an organized game on (or, at least, not more than one because of its [small] size). The adults are fairly hands off.*

This observer reported that institutional contexts affected play activities and engagement. Although students were running and getting physical exercise, no options were available for students who did not want to run and play tag. The tag game they were playing, which was boys against girls, was not always safe. The field notes from this recess period also contain notations of pushing and aggressive tagging that went along with this game and were not dealt with by the adults at recess. The game spanned the grass and blacktop areas, instead of having its own space, which made it a hazard for everyone else in the space who wasn't playing. For these very young children, the lack of adult engagement was problematic.

The absence of discipline problems might be seen as an indicator of a good recess, but that is not always the case. We saw examples of recess that were simply unexciting. For example, at another school, recess included minimal activities and students wandered around in groups, but no sustained games or play was observed. The field notes report:

> *A lot of students just wandered around and were not active. The monitors did not engage much with the students.... There was not much negative language, but there also wasn't much positive during recess time. The aides and teachers when they come out to get the students focus on threatening students with punishments for not lining up properly.*

This recess was underwhelming although some students did play a little and others did get physical exercise. Students' attitudes appeared to match the lackluster enthusiasm of the adults at recess and the lack of institutional support for recess. There was not enough engagement at this recess for it to be a place where most students can practice their social and emotional skills and be physically active or engaged in play. With more attention to planning, this recess could have been turned around so that it was a fun and engaged time.

Across all the recess observations, we noted behaviors that were inconsistent with the goals of an engaged recess that supports students' learning. Observers noted many instances of students holding, but not using, playground equipment like balls and jump ropes, or using this equipment in potentially unsafe ways—for instance, dragging other children around using jump ropes and hula hoops. We heard many students using inappropriate language that one would not expect to hear on an elementary school campus, and we even witnessed a boy urinating in a field rather than using the bathroom. We saw children getting hurt and play fighting that bordered on real fighting, often without any adult attention or intervention. Yard monitors were not always engaged with children, helping them to resolve problems or stepping in to check on a child who was crying. We did observe some monitors who were clearly invested in their jobs and engaged with children, but we also observed many who congregated with the other monitors as well as those who sat idly on benches while chaos surrounded them.

Alongside these examples of what wasn't working, we saw some great examples of what did work. At a school that had tapped some recess monitors to act as coaches to get students engaged in games and support their play, it was a different experience for children. The field notes read:

> *This recess was really well organized with four main activities and a lot of choice. Nearly all children were involved in an activity. The female paraprofessional played with the kids, was encouraging, and used positive language, and there was limited conflict (some arguing at basketball). Kids lined up easily and quickly when they were told recess was over.*

The principal of this school, Roberta Robinson, had been a staff member for almost twenty years at Lawrence Hogan Elementary, an urban school located across the street from the local parole and probation office. It was her second year as principal, and Ms. Robinson was aiming to make improvements to recess at the school. She had decided to lengthen the lunch period by fifteen minutes so students could have time to play after their thirty-minute lunch. She brought in the local Parks and Recreation Department to lead physical education–like activities for students during their class time. And she hired a paraprofessional staff member to organize games and support children at recess. Principal Robinson described her recess philosophy as follows:

> *We talk about children being well-rounded, you know; they can't just live on reading, math, writing, you know, and science and social studies, but that health piece, good eating, good minds on how to deal with things, but also that physical exertion—children need that. . . . If they're racing, if they're doing competitive sports, it can teach them good sportsmanship because it's not always about winning. You know, you're learning some strategies. . . . If you're playing basketball out on the court, okay, you have a position that you're playing; there's a reason that you need to play that position.*

Before these changes, whether the students had recess was up to their individual teachers, so some students had daily recess and others had recess two times a week or less. Principal Robinson felt that a more organized and equitable approach to recess would provide more opportunities for physical activity for her students and was looking to make changes to support these goals. Field notes from the second- and third-grade recess at Hogan show students engaged in a range of activities, including football, basketball, and jump rope. Some of the games were integrated by gender and others were not, and adults supported students by playing with them and encouraging them, modeling inclusive behavior. Although Principal Robinson did not set out to create a positive school climate or boost students' social and emotional learning or connection to adults, through her attention to recess activities, she was able to accomplish these multiple goals at this recess period.

Behavior and Discipline Issues at Recess

Discipline and punishment interact with students' recess time in two main ways. The first is that recess can be withheld from individual students or entire classes for a variety of reasons, ranging from misbehavior to incomplete class work. Instead of being on the play yard at recess, students can be kept inside in a classroom, the lunchroom, or a separate detention room. Having students sit out at recess—where they are physically present on the play yard but not allowed to play—is also common, particularly if the misbehavior for which they are being punished happens on the play yard. The second way recess and discipline interact is that recess altercations are often the source of disciplinary referrals to the office. Students can be disciplined in a variety of ways for misbehavior during recess time, depending on school culture, the seriousness of the disciplinary incident, and who is monitoring recess at that time. Using recess withholding as punishment and dealing with disciplinary incidents that stem from recess are both important considerations for schools, and they handle these tricky problems in different ways.

Recess Withholding as Punishment

Just as we observed at Principal Johnson's inner-city school, the majority (79 percent) of principals surveyed in the Gallup/RWJF poll reported that recess is taken away as punishment in their school, and about half (54 percent) reported that recess is also given as a reward. Because surveyed principals described that recess is offered nearly every day at their schools, when recess is used as a reward, typically the teacher would take students out for an extra recess during class time.

Why, you might wonder, is withholding recess used as a punishment when its benefits are so important to children? Withholding recess is considered a strong mechanism for eliciting better student behavior because it is the period of the day that students value most. Threats to remove recess are believed to incentivize students to behave the way teachers want, but no real evidence supports the efficacy of this approach. Research has documented the strong positive effects of recess on student outcomes, but I have not found any studies that demonstrate the efficacy of withholding recess on any student outcomes, including behavior. It seems that this is more assumption than fact.

Across the twelve schools we visited that were not formally implementing recess reforms, we observed recess being withheld from students in eight schools. When I say that we observed this, what I mean is that students were physically separated from play at recess time, and we were able to see that they were not allowed to play. We learned through interviews and other conversations that in some cases schools had separate detention rooms so that students who were punished never left the school building, in which case we did not observe them having recess withheld (and these instances are not accounted for in our observations). In these eight schools I describe next, we could see students sitting out or knew that they were kept inside in the lunchroom instead of being let out to recess. We were not always aware of the reasons for their punishment, but most commonly students sat out due to classroom, lunchroom, before-school (including on the bus), or recess misbehavior. Teachers, administrators, and lunch and recess monitors all have authority and discretion to hold a child out of recess. We did not hear of any schools that had common guidelines for how this punishment should be administered, in terms of behaviors that should be punished and length of recess withdrawal.

As is shown in figure 2.3, half (eighteen) of these thirty-six recess periods involved students sitting out for punishment of some kind.[5] In most cases, the full class was not held back from recess, but rather between two and fifteen students across an entire recess period were sitting out for anywhere between five minutes and the entire period. Schools typically

FIGURE 2.3   Extent of recess withholding across twelve schools

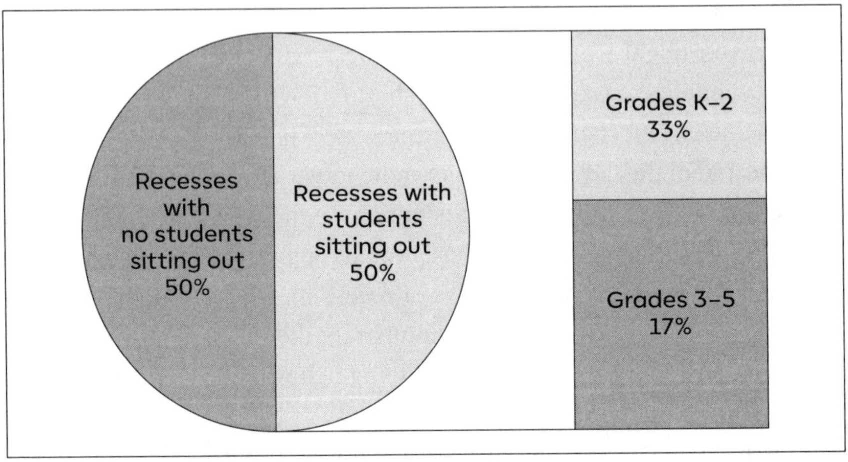

Recesses with no students sitting out 50%

Recesses with students sitting out 50%

Grades K–2 33%

Grades 3–5 17%

Source: Observations of thirty-six recesses in twelve schools nationwide

have an area that students are sent for punishment—against a wall, next to the bathroom, or on a certain bench. Children of all ages, but especially the youngest students, had recess withheld in this group of schools. In the twenty recesses that served children in kindergarten, first, and second grade, twelve (60 percent) had students sitting out due to punishment. In contrast, in the sixteen recesses serving older students in third, fourth, and fifth grades, six (38 percent) had students sitting out for punishment. In three instances entire classes were kept inside at recess, including one where all the kindergarten, first-, and second-grade students who were supposed to be at recess that day were not allowed to leave the lunchroom to play outside, at a lunchroom monitor's discretion, because of misbehavior. Both girls and boys were subject to recess withholding, although we observed more boys than girls sitting out. Particularly where ten or more students were sitting out at once, it was usually the case that the number of boys exceeded the number of girls.

Again, as a reminder, these examples of recess withholding occurred on days that were scheduled in advance and when we were visiting schools for the main purpose of observing recess. I do not believe they were anomalous recess circumstances because experience tells me that school personnel want to make their best impression on the day that outsiders come to visit their schools.

Principals Johnson and Robinson described very different recess approaches, and it's clear that in Principal Robinson's urban school, moments of success were achieved with the changes she put in place. However, both of these schools withheld recess as a means of punishing students. On the one day we visited, Principal Johnson's school had two recess periods for two different grade-level groupings, and at both entire classes were not let out to recess. Principal Robinson, who had worked so hard to lengthen the recess period and train paraprofessionals to play with students and organize games, had four recess periods that day with different combinations of student grade levels. At one of these periods, an entire class of kindergarteners had recess withheld. At all but the second- and third-grade recess, which is the one that my research team felt was among the best we observed, students were sitting out, having been punished for things like running on the blacktop or missing schoolwork.

The extensive use of this form of punishment, even in schools that are actively trying to improve their recess environments, is counterproductive. Although there is no research base that examines the effects of withholding recess, there is research on punishment and discipline in schools more broadly.[6] School discipline is considered transactional—that is, a combination of adults' expectations, students' understanding of those expectations, and school climate, to name a few. The research indicates that punishment that excludes students can have unexpected detrimental effects, such as worsening behavior even further by having misbehaving students sit out together. When educators withhold a recess from children as punishment, they lose an opportunity to help students better understand the expectations of the school and to help students practice the social and emotional skills they need to be successful at recess. They also message to students that they don't belong with the other students, that their behavior sets them apart, which students can internalize and then perpetuate the cycle. For students who are caught up in a full-class recess punishment, they learn that other students' misbehavior can lead to their own recess punishment because not every student in a class that has recess withheld is actually misbehaving. What does this message tell students who are trying hard to behave?

My sense from the many teachers and principals I have interviewed in this work is that the students who individually have recess withheld are often the repeat offenders, those whose behavior needs correcting day after day. I have no doubt that children with serious behavioral problems tax their teachers' and recess monitors' patience and perhaps even create safety problems for other children at recess. But the repeated withholding of recess for small and large offenses has not been studied or shown to support better future student behavior. There are alternatives to withholding recess, which will be discussed further in chapter 4.

Behavioral Issues and Discipline at Recess

Even in the diverse set of schools by geographic location and socioeconomic status of its students covered in the Gallup/RWJF survey, the problem of discipline at recess time is nearly universal. Principals do not report excessive numbers of these problems, but persistent ones. The majority of principals want to pay attention to recess because it's where most of their disciplinary referrals originate; 88 percent of principals responded that discipline-related problems occur most commonly outside of classroom time, and recess is cited by 90 percent of principals as the key nonclassroom location in which disciplinary incidents occur. As is shown in figure 2.4, almost half of principals in urban low-income schools had at least occasional problems with fighting, whereas 27 percent of principals from other schools had this problem at least occasionally. According to principals, bullying and teasing were about as common in urban low-income schools as they were in other schools, with the majority of principals reporting they had at least occasional problems with each.

Student behavioral problems at recess are ubiquitous; we expect to see conflicts that arise in normal play—like who goes first in a game or whether the ball is in or out. Learning how to resolve these conflicts is part of students' social development, and learning to control one's temper and move beyond disappointment at losing a game or not playing well is part of emotional development. Some students may come to recess with these developmental milestones conquered, and they can and should resolve

FIGURE 2.4 Percent of principals reporting occasional or more regular disciplinary incidents at recess

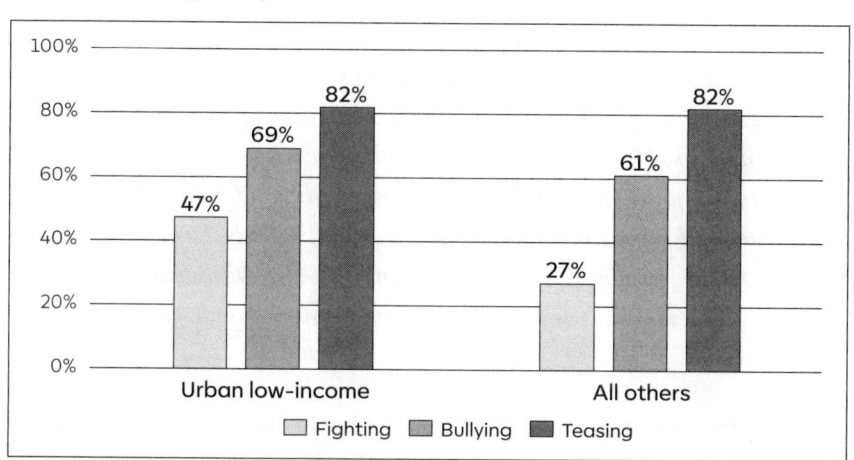

Source: Gallup/RWJF survey of principals

their own conflicts. Others, however, may still be learning, and for these learners, if the adults who supervise recess do not attend to these problems, they can quickly escalate into much bigger issues that students may not be able to resolve on their own and that can affect student safety. Schools can support social and emotional development through recess planning in many ways; putting into place these preventive measures can also improve behavior and reduce disciplinary incidents at recess. Adult supervisors, especially, play a large role in student engagement and safety at recess.

A complex combination of student social and emotional development combined with school, family, and neighborhood factors as well as school climate come together in school disciplinary incidents. The worst disciplinary incident we observed at any of the twelve schools was in a third-grade recess period. Field notes indicate a fight broke out among two boys.

> There is some tag going on between two other boys. They are swearing at each other. After five minutes of this, it turns into a fist fight. At first they are both upright, holding on to each other's shirts and arms, punching each other in the head and body. A crowd of twenty students begins to surround them. The white male adult [recess

> monitor] tries to intervene by saying, "Hey! Stop it!" and reaching out to separate them, but he can't. He is now behind and outside the crowd and just watches. The boys are now on the ground on the asphalt/parking lot hitting each other in the face and stomach with fists. I can hear the contact. The male adult watches them with his arms crossed for at least a minute. He then sees an opening and grabs the flailed arm of one of the boys and drags him away while telling the other students to go play. I can't tell if it is the victim or the perpetrator. The other boy is absorbed into the crowd and they disperse. The female adult [recess monitor] did not get up from the bench.

Due to unforeseen circumstances, we were unable to interview the school principal, Ms. White, on that same day, but we followed up and conducted a phone interview later that week. Having already observed this incident, the interviewer asked a standard question on our interview protocol: "Do you feel like there's a problem with conflict at recess time or out on the playground or at lunchtime?" Principal White responded, "Not too much." Our interviewer persisted, "When it happens, what does it look like?" And then Principal White admitted that this was actually a problem at her school:

> Well, there was... well, they sometimes actually get into a fight, a physical fight. Or, sometimes, it can be an argument. They're not very frequent, but that's one of the things that we've been talking about, if the supervision is adequate and diligent, that it's a proactive measure and preventing some of the altercations.

Probing even further, the interviewer asked Principal White what she does when this kind of incident occurs. She responded that she uses a version of a talk-it-out approach, trying to mediate the problem, but that also she might separate the children or sit them out of recess. Principal White was not present at school on the day the fight broke out, and we have no way of knowing how it was ultimately resolved, whether the two boys were brought to the office, if their parents were called, if adults had mediated whatever had caused the disagreement.

No other recess period we observed included such a violent outbreak of aggression. Instead, at most schools we observed activities that observers referred to as roughhousing, horseplay, and play fighting, what developmental psychologists call rough-and-tumble play. Although play fighting is part of a normal developmental process, sometimes it was hard for us as observers—and also the students—to tell if the interactions were play or real. For instance, in this interaction the observer thought the play has possibly crossed a line:

> *There is a good amount of play fighting or horsing mostly among boys: six boys are horsing around together; five boys are horsing around or play fighting; one boy and two girls horse around; one boy [lying] on the ground pretends to cry. Another boy kicks him when is on the ground. Play fight?*

We also observed quite a bit of pushing, shoving, and touching mostly among students who were playing games like tag or those who were not actively engaged in a game, and similarly while students were waiting in line to go out to recess or back into school after recess. These interactions often went unnoticed and therefore had the potential to escalate, but in some cases monitors admonished students to keep their hands to themselves or said "no touching." Pushing in line was sometimes punished by withholding recess, or delaying it until students could stand still, a nearly impossible task for thirty elementary students at once.

Even where we did not observe any conflicts or problems at recess, principals acknowledged that disciplinary issues at recess were problematic at their schools. In some schools it was clear that the problem was pervasive throughout the student body, or students in specific grade levels. In other schools, however, we learned that problems among only a few students created recess issues for many others. For instance, at one school, the principal described the problems at recess like this:

> *I don't see it with a lot of students, but the students who I do see it with, it's an issue that it's typically the same students over and over again.... It's typically over being extremely competitive, over, you know, who kicked a goal and who didn't, and who scored and who didn't....*

At another school, the principal also talked about the difference between normal conflict that arises during play and the problems that can be attributed to only a handful of children at recess:

> *Now, there's arguments about whether or not something was fair or a rule was followed or a rule was broken. . . . But sometimes, people say "They chased me," "They pushed me down," . . . So, it's not . . . I mean, it's not ferocious kind of stuff out there. . . . But there are individual kids who really do have a lot of significant aggression issues and maybe other kinds of issues going on too. And they do target kids; they'll hurt kids.*

In my travels through elementary recess, I have heard again and again that a few children in a grade can disrupt activities for everyone else on the play yard or in the classroom. Principals have shared with me that the same three of four students are sent to their office week after week. But this is not an impenetrable problem. Giving tools to students who are often at the center of recess conflict to turn their behavior around and become positive leaders is among the most effective ways to address the disciplinary issues of a particular student. Plus, planning and supporting a recess environment that engages all students in productive recess activities is the best way to combat many of the play yard challenges faced by these elementary schools.

As I've said, what adults do at recess also matters because discipline can be thought of as a transaction between the student and the adult. One principal described how sometimes the adults at his school were not living up to their task:

> *Certainly, there are times when the kid doesn't . . . the kid will talk to an adult and the adult doesn't take it seriously enough, just says, "Stay away from them," or whatever, and it turns out that that student really needed more help than that and that didn't happen.*

How adults handle their monitoring responsibilities is an important factor in how active and engaged students are and the extent of disciplinary problems that occur during recess. If students feel unsafe or their recess environment is chaotic, this feeling degrades school climate and students learn to distrust, rather than to trust, the adults charged with keeping them safe.

Adult Supervision and Interaction with Students at Recess

Adult recess monitors play an important role at recess. They set the tone for recess and have the potential to model prosocial behavior for students, engage with students to build relationships, and support students when conflict arises so that children feel physically and emotionally safe. When adults engage with students in positive ways, they can improve recess for both children and themselves.

At the recesses we observed at twelve schools nationwide, the majority of recess monitors were paraprofessionals who worked part-time at the school. In some schools, administrators also were present at recess although they were not consistently out at consecutive recesses, nor did they always stay for the entire period because their multiple roles at school did not allow for them to always be present. At the two schools with two recesses per day, teachers monitored the shorter morning recess, and paraprofessionals monitored students at lunch recess. We learned that some of the paraprofessionals were hired only for lunch and recess duty, while others had other positions, such as crossing guards or classroom aides. With their limited hours, these staff were generally not provided any formal training or professional development to do their jobs.

An ideal recess environment would have sufficient staffing for some recess monitors to focus on engaging students in play and others to make sure students are feeling safe and following school rules. However, the recesses we observed in the twelve schools did not have staffing levels that allowed for this kind of division of responsibility. In most cases, the student to monitor ratio was about 50:1, but there were examples of both more and less adult presence at recess. Indeed, in the Gallup/RWJF poll of principals, increasing the number of recess monitors was the number one priority principals reported for improving their recesses.

Even so, we observed many examples of adult monitors playing with children while also trying to do the other parts of their job. For example, at one school, the recess monitor played a game called "tap" with students. The field notes read:

> *The kids who played "tap" with the monitor had a good time and were engaged and sustained as long as she stayed there. But when she left, the game waned. She kept leaving and coming back.*

Presumably this monitor was leaving and returning because she was responsible for keeping an eye on other parts of the recess yard in addition to the location of the tap game. Students enjoy playing with adults, and her presence aided the continuation of the game.

At another school, the yard monitor, Ms. Lizzie, spent the majority of her time with a large group of older boys playing basketball on a court that was separated from the rest of the yard. We learned that basketball was only allowed to proceed at that school with an adult present because it had been so rife with conflict. Ms. Lizzie took it upon herself to referee for the two teams, and the play had the feel of a serious basketball game. The field notes indicate that she was not playing with the boys, but she was "playing a vital role in supporting their play by acting as referee, keeping score, and keeping the game going." She cheered for the teams: "That's what I'm talking about . . . There you go!" She also admonished them to play fair: "There are other players. Don't be cheating. Pass the ball." The game was intense and conflict arose, but she called a jump ball when needed and quieted the students who disagreed with her calls.

Ms. Lizzie was very actively involved, but others engaged more quietly with students to support their play. We saw numerous examples of yard monitors turning long jump ropes so students (mainly girls) could jump in. They sometimes cheered for students and made sure everyone had a turn. We also saw examples of male monitors playing football or basketball with students, an administrator engaging in a game of dodgeball with students, and another playing kickball. It was not always the case that monitors stayed with the game for the entire recess, but their presence in the game encouraged students to join.

Unfortunately, not all recesses had engaged or positive monitors. We also observed recesses where monitors sat on benches, talked among themselves, checked their phones, or yelled at children. For example, at the same school where Ms. Lizzie's basketball game was well monitored, the rest of recess was not. The remaining monitors stood in one place and talked to each other without engaging much with students. No specific training or expectations had been provided to encourage them to engage with students.

At another school, the adult monitors were not tuned in to what was happening with the students. The field notes read:

> *The two lunch monitors walk around, occasionally engage with kids, tell them to clean up, and largely ignore the bullying and running around that is happening all around them. There was one kid punching another kid in front of another adult, and he did nothing.*

At a different school, recess monitors were present but also not engaged. The field notes similarly read:

> *These two [monitors] are talking to each other, one with her back to the blacktop, watching the structure, one with her back to the structure, watching the blacktop. There is another female adult here who walks around a little more, watches kickball. Overall, they are pretty hands off and don't engage the kids much.*

These monitors seemed as if they were paying attention to what was happening around them, but they were not attempting to build relationships with students, support their engagement, or model prosocial behavior for students. These are missed opportunities for creating positive recess environments. However, things could be even worse. We observed a handful of recesses where monitors were mean to children, yelling at them instead of helping them, and ignoring students who got hurt. At the same school where the fistfight broke out, the field notes from earlier in recess read:

> *I observe the other [yard monitor] talking to a small boy, berating, "What is the problem?? Take the shoe off and quit whining!!" I also observe one [monitor] screaming at two kids, never leaving the bench. She called them by name and yelled, "NO!" These adults exclusively*

> sat on the benches and watched, eating a snack, checking phones, and yelling at kids from their seats. One adult got up at one point and was interacting with some kids but ignored a kid being kicked in the head and crying and some other mean teasing in close proximity.

At another school, the school resource officer (a police officer stationed at the school) supervised recess along with the other monitors. Although the resource officer is charged solely with student safety, this officer was actually more responsive to students than the other recess monitors. Still, his approach only went so far, according to field notes:

> Most of their interactions seem to be pretty rough. Even Officer Smith had a gruff exchange with a student who was crying before coming out to recess, telling him to stop crying. Yes, they stopped physical conflicts that were happening, at least most of the time. However, it only involved stopping the physical violence and didn't really resolve the conflict. For example, [I] heard a kid on the way in from recess saying that he heard someone was going to get beaten up.

A Focus on Great Recess for All

The descriptions of what happens at a typical recess indicate large variations both across and even within schools in recess operations and student engagement. Two key factors stand out as important: (1) the actions and attitudes of recess monitors and (2) access to daily recess for all children. These factors also both came out in the Gallup/RWJF survey of principals, but in different ways.

In the Gallup/RWJF survey, principals reported that the one most important thing they could do to improve recess was related to the role of the recess monitors (figure 2.5). For instance, 29 percent said they wanted more monitors, 18 percent said training for playground management, 10 percent responded better supervision, and another 5 percent wanted more volunteers. In total, 62 percent of principals felt that having more or better trained staff was the highest priority change they could make to improve recess.

FIGURE 2.5   Principals' reports of most important thing to be done to improve recess

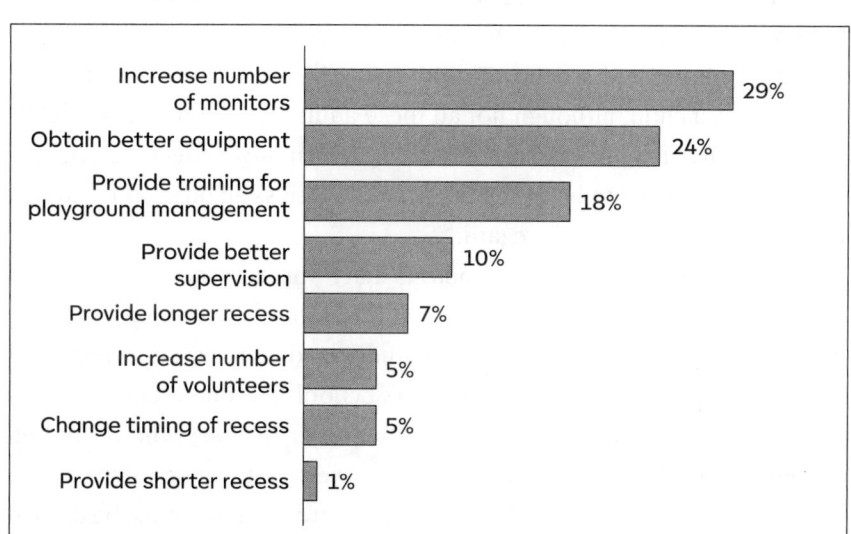

Source: Gallup/RWJF survey of principals

Our data from twelve schools that entered into a lottery to receive the recess reform program but were delayed implementation help to explain this emphasis on staffing. We observed that in recesses where adults played with children or were somehow involved with their play by turning jump ropes or acting as a referee, students were much more likely to be engaged in and sustain their play in games. When adults walked away to attend to other duties, these games were often not sustained. Recesses that included adults who modeled positive language by cheering for students or helping them to cheer for each other and those that included adult monitors who encouraged children to play also saw greater student engagement. The recess periods with the least student engagement and the most conflict were ones where adult monitors treated students negatively or ignored them.

Surprisingly, none of the principal respondents to the survey indicated that ensuring daily recess for all children would be the biggest improvement to recess. Administrators and staff at the schools we visited viewed recess withdrawal as a valid punishment for large and small infractions and used it frequently, even with the youngest students. We were not made aware of guidelines at any of the twelve schools for appropriate use of recess withholding, either individually or for an entire class. Teachers, administrators, recess monitors, and lunchroom monitors all had discretion to remove recess from a child, although not all these adults have knowledge of children's personal lives or classroom challenges that might affect their behavior. There appeared to be little coordination, unless an office referral was made, among adults in this regard.

The bottom line about recess today is that it varies tremendously school by school and even recess by recess within schools. Principal Johnson's urban school struggled to even allow students to be released to recess on the day we visited. Principal Robinson's school had one recess that was the best recess we observed anywhere but other recesses where children sat out for small infractions and monitors were not paying attention. To ensure a high-quality recess for all students, yard monitors must be trained in play yard management, student engagement, conflict resolution, and alternatives to recess withholding. Most principals know this but also face barriers to accessing the resources they need. However, having more and better trained staff is only the beginning. School leaders need a clear vision or road map forward, a plan they can rally around, with research that inspires confidence.

PART II

Improving Recess for All Children

CHAPTER THREE

Organizing and Customizing Recess

Educators agree that recess is an important time in the school day that has the potential to support growth for students in all developmental areas. When schools are intentional about planning their recess programs, they can create an organized, inclusive, and supported recess that helps to build and solidify students' social and emotional skills and at the same time encourage play and physical activity. With school recess plans in place and operating as expected, students can experience a positive recess culture—one that builds connections among students and with adults, supports inclusion, encourages conflict resolution, and helps students to sustain their play so they can return to class feeling satisfied and happy. The extent and type of recess plan that schools adopt will vary based on a variety of factors, including school facilities, students' interests, the bell schedule, available staffing, and others. This chapter offers a set of first steps that any school can take to begin the process of customizing recess, using few resources, in an effort to improve the recess culture.

In this chapter, I introduce the concept of "organized recess," that is, a recess where specific games occupy dedicated spaces in the play yard, equipment is managed centrally, and common rules to games are established to promote fair play. Is this a so-called structured recess where children lose their ability to play what they like, including imaginary or creative games? Absolutely not. The approach I describe is based on a philosophy that recess should be tailored to the school context—the space, needs, and play culture of the school. My key argument is that planning for how the recess space and time are used can support greater freedom of play for students and more student engagement, as well as improved feelings of safety and satisfaction for both students and school staff.

This flexible approach to recess organization is essential because school context varies tremendously across and even within regions. In an East Coast urban elementary school that I visited, for instance, the recess yard was small and oblong shaped, filled mainly with blacktop but with a small corner of grass that was large enough for students to kick or throw a ball, but not large to engage in a full soccer or football game. This school also had a small round court with a knee-height brick wall around it off to one side that, on first glance, did not seem to lend itself to any kinds of games, and there was a big puddle in the middle of the blacktop. The school did not have a fixed play structure for climbing or swinging but did have some markings on the blacktop—a map of the city, four-square, and hopscotch. Figuring out what to play and where to play it was the primary challenge of this space. Soccer and tag were popular at this school, but in the small space, children in both games felt crowded by those in the other.

Halfway across the country in the mountain region, I visited a brand new charter school located in an office park. This school had no play structure and had no play yard at all. Recess was held in a section of an asphalt parking lot, cordoned off with yellow tape from the school staff's parked cars. The parking lot was not landscaped with children in mind, including an unfortunately large number of decorative round rocks that were the perfect size for small hands to pick up and throw. Without intentional recess planning and equipment, there would be no obvious games to play or productive activities in which students could engage.

Even further west in a West Coast elementary school I visited, space was abundant. A large blacktop area had markings for four four-square courts, six basketball nets, a wall for wall ball, and five tetherball courts.

The school also had a grassy field with a baseball diamond on one end and a walking path around it. In addition, two newer-looking play structures had opportunities for climbing and monkey bars. Counter to what one might imagine, figuring out what to play and where to play it was also a challenge at this school. The issue here, as the principal described in an interview, was that the students could not agree on how to play the games and therefore were unable to play. He said, "One of the biggest things about this community when I came here is that the kids really didn't know how to play and play well together, and they weren't engaged in games." Although this school had plenty of space to play a variety of games, students needed some assistance in learning to start and sustain games on their own.

Each of these schools faced challenges and opportunities at recess and had a need for improved recess planning, but what that planning entailed differed. Principals at each of these three schools recognized that recess was not living up to its potential and felt they needed some guidance to improve their school's recess culture. Student behavior does not exist in a vacuum; the culture of recess at a school shapes how the children engage at recess. Many components go into improving recess culture, but I am starting first with recess organization.

Organizing recess is the most important step for creating a culture of play and improving student outcomes as well as overall school climate. By making small and low-cost changes to recess operations, schools can garner huge benefits that will be noticeable to students, teachers, recess monitors, and administrators. In the year we visited, all three of these schools were able to organize their recess yards and create spaces for student engagement in play, but the key was to tailor the recess organization to the individual school environment.

Against the Extremes of Structured and Unstructured Recess

Discussions of recess organization often trigger reactions from those on both sides of the structured versus unstructured recess debate. What has come to be known as a structured recess is one in which an adult controls the game or games that students are allowed to play and leads them in activities. Structured recess does not allow for student choice and restricts children who want to engage in free or imaginative play from doing so, with programming something akin to a physical education class. In contrast, an unstructured recess is one governed entirely by free choice. Students can engage in any activity they choose, and adults do not lead games although they might help students to set them up if needed. Equipment might be available for children or perhaps not, but the goal is for children to use their imaginations and creativity to create their own fun at recess. This division of structured and unstructured recess is a false dichotomy in many ways. Certainly, some schools embrace one or the other, but many schools fall somewhere in between the two, and many others have no official recess philosophy at all.

Philosophical differences in what are the perceived goals of recess underpin much of the two camps' perspectives. For example, public health specialists concerned with children's cardiovascular health and obesity tout recess as an opportunity for moderate to vigorous physical activity (MVPA) that is a necessary input to children's ongoing health. The research conducted by these professionals focuses largely on structured recess. They argue that schools are an ideal setting for students to accrue some of the sixty minutes of physical activity recommended by the American Academy of Pediatrics because children do not always have these opportunities outside of school. Especially for children whose communities are not conducive to active play after school, recess can be the place where those activities happen. Abundant evidence supports the belief that introducing structured physical activity breaks to recess or other times in the school day increases students' MVPA.[1] Because these studies tend to be focused on physical health outcomes rather than the other developmental outcomes that schools support, it is unclear whether structured recess also helps students to develop social and emotional skills such as self-regulation, conflict resolution, and cooperation. One might assume that structured recess does not support social and emotional development because these skills grow through peer-to-peer and peer-to-adult interaction and negotiation. A structured recess may offer fewer of these opportunities, but research is not adequate to draw conclusions at this point.

Unstructured play, according to developmental psychologists, is how children learn. By using their imaginations, being spontaneous, negotiating with other children, and finding activities to occupy their time on their own, children learn and grow in ways that are not possible through structured activities. Some evidence supports the belief that unstructured play can also be physically active. For instance, research in Australia has considered what happens when moveable and recycled items that you might not normally find at a school (e.g., milk crates, car tires) are introduced into an unstructured school recess environment.[2] This simple intervention led to increases in young children's activity levels and, according to teachers, also improved their social skills, creativity, and resilience on the play yard.

On the other hand, much of the research that identifies the benefits of structured recess on physical health outcomes uses unstructured recess as a control condition, so there is also considerable evidence that unstructured time does not generate the same physical health benefits as more structured time. One opposing position comes from University of the Arts professor Anna Beresin, who has studied student activity in recess through observation and art activities. In one study, she found—in a small sample of students—that unstructured recess supported more physical activity (in terms of steps per minute) than the more structured physical education class. She explained, "Much of the gym time in the current study was spent waiting, or observing other children doing an activity.... In contrast, on the playground, the children linked their movements to the activities and transitioned themselves physically, creating a collage of activity."[3]

Neither of these camps specifically addresses the school contextual factors that might make either structured or unstructured recess more plausible or successful. Issues such as the demographics of the school, the type of neighborhood in which it is located, and whether its students are meeting state standards for academics are hardly mentioned in this body of work, but these factors underpin the recess experience for schools. For example, psychologist Anthony Pellegrini, according to notes in his 2006 book, conducted much of his research in schools that serve predominantly white children.[4] The Australian studies that introduced recycled materials did not include detailed enough descriptions of the school contexts to demonstrate that these were approaches that would work with all student populations. In contrast, Beresin's work took place in inner-city Philadelphia, and in her 2014 book, she shared stories of unpredictable recess environments that yielded conflict.[5] School context matters, and I don't know that putting wooden crates and car tires in every play yard would have the same effects as it did in the Australian studies. I can imagine that in some other contexts, adding materials like these in a fully unstructured environment might result in added chaos and physical altercations, but we do not have the research available to tell us if this is so.

The literature points to benefits of both structured and unstructured recesses, but why can't these positive qualities, which lead to many good outcomes, coexist? Is recess really meant to be fully structured or fully unstructured? The answer is no, because different children need different recess experiences to achieve the midday break that helps them to reset and go back to class ready to learn. I argue that schools most need an approach to recess that combines the best of the structured and unstructured approaches, one that supports physical activity as well as social and emotional development.

Organized Recess: A Flexible Way to Improve Recess

Recess, like any other time of the school day, requires some planning. My research findings demonstrate that schools can create a positive recess environment through planning and organization that is neither structured nor unstructured and that supports both physical activity and social and emotional growth. It is not a simple one-size-fits-all approach, but rather a customized approach to recess planning and organization that requires firsthand knowledge of the school context and the students' needs—information that all school administrators already have. Given the potential benefits and drawbacks of both structured and unstructured recess approaches, and the multiple ways that schools can support students to develop, this hybrid approach of organized recess makes the most sense and has been proven to be effective.

When I first began conducting research in partnership with Playworks, organizational leaders were having an internal debate about the words to use when talking about their approach. Adding "structure" had become akin to implementing a rigid structured recess, which was not what they were doing. We needed a better descriptor that more accurately evoked the sort of guidance the program was providing to both children and staff at recess. After thoughtful consideration, the concept of "organized recess" was born.

In an organized recess, set games are introduced with common rules and predictable locations. These games are possibly even led by adults, for those who want to participate. Free choice is also available so that students who do not want to engage in the available games can have creative and imaginary time, climb on a play structure, *or* read a book if that's how they want to spend their break time.

> **In an organized recess**
>
> - Games have common rules and are set up in predictable locations.
> - Each game has its own space, and students playing other games do not run through.
> - Students have free choice in what to do.
> - Space is available for creative or imaginary games.
> - Equipment is available for play.
> - Adults support student play.
> - Games are inclusive.

Research shows that recess organization can have positive effects on children. For instance, a randomized controlled trial in Belgium introduced game equipment with activity cards that teachers could use to help students use the equipment. Over the course of three months, findings indicated increased MVPA for children in the intervention schools relative to those who did not have game equipment introduced.[6] Another study focused on creating playground zones, including one for active sports, another for other activities, and a third quiet zone, along with fixed equipment such as basketball nets and soccer goals.[7] Students at schools with these changes experienced increases in their MVPA over the long term, compared to students at other comparable schools without these changes. This study included a costly overhaul of school play yards, but less costly, simpler changes can also make a difference for students. A study of schools in a lower-income area of Melbourne, Australia, indicated that simple changes such as having equipment and painting markings for games on the blacktop surface, combined with teacher presence on the play yard, increased physical activity among children at recess.[8]

Notably, none of these studies focuses on how play yard organization affects outcomes other than physical activity, which is a limitation of the field as a whole. Published research supports the effectiveness of recess organization, paired with other supports for social and emotional learning, on students' physical activity—especially for girls and students from ethnically underrepresented backgrounds—and social and emotional outcomes, including adult-peer relationships and conflict resolution skills.[9] My own research demonstrates that in addition to physical activity, recess organization alone improves student engagement and enjoyment. With an organized recess, students have more opportunity to engage in activities with peers and adults, students and adults find recess to be more manageable and fun, children spend more time being physically active, and they gain important social and emotional skills that transfer back to the classroom.

Eight Steps to Organizing Recess

Trimbull School is an urban K–8 school on the East Coast. It has an oblong play yard with a small grassy field and an odd round-shaped court. When my team visited Trimbull, it was a "turnaround" school, meaning much of its staff had been reconstituted due to student performance on standardized tests. The school had a new principal, two new assistant principals, and a sea of newly hired young teachers brought in through the turnaround effort.

The school, which served a majority of African American students, had lengthened the school day so that with the bus ride to and from school, in winter students might not see the light of day during school. Except at recess. Playworks worked with this school to provide a daily coach who was available not just at recess, but throughout the school day and even after school to lead games with students and support them in play. When we met Coach Kim, she had spent the year figuring out how to organize the odd-shaped play yard, describing her role as follows:

So, I offer opportunities for the kids to play at recess in a way that's—we don't like to say "structured," because then people think that we're forcing the kids to play, it's definitely not. They have a choice of different activities they can choose, and sometimes they don't choose any of the activities, and it's up to them—but it's a way to make it a less chaotic, safe place for the kids, where there's play that's going on that's meaningful.

> **Eight steps to organizing recess**
>
> 1. Assess the landscape.
> 2. Assess recess policies.
> 3. Explore the play culture.
> 4. Engage in low-cost updates.
> 5. Provide necessary loose equipment.
> 6. Centralize equipment checkout.
> 7. Map the play yard.
> 8. Roll out the format to adults and students.

Each grade level had its own recess at this school, which was necessary because the space was not large enough for combined recesses. Each recess had its own set of games based on what Coach Kim saw the students liked to play. For instance, in the first-grade recess we observed games like bucketball (basketball with smaller buckets that elementary students can reach), soccer, jump rope, and a tag game called "fishy fishy." When fifth graders were out, they used the space differently. Bucketball was still popular, but there was a volleyball game happening (without a net), and kids were playing kickball, wall ball, and gaga ball—an Israeli game meant to be played in a round court! With very little grass and a small play space, how did Trimbull students manage to pack in all those games? The key was organization.

One of the first things Coach Kim did when she started at Trimbull in the fall was to organize the yard into spaces to be used for certain games. The round-shaped court was perfect for a mini soccer game or for gaga ball, which she introduced to students as the year progressed. She designated space for wall ball and assigned the space just outside the school doors for football. She created lanes along one side of the yard for a track that could support students who wanted to walk and talk, or races for those who wanted to run. The bucketball hoops were located centrally, and she worked with students to help them keep their other games out of that space. There were predictable places in the yard that students could gather to find the games they liked. For students who were not interested in those games, they could explore other spaces to play tag, do gymnastics, or create their own imaginative play.

What Coach Kim did was to organize the recess so that play could happen in a more unencumbered way. She organized to maximize student engagement in play, and all the changes Coach Kim put in place that year were with that goal in mind. This result did not just happen though. Coach Kim was intentional in her process, which led to successful outcomes for her students.

I've broken down the organization process into eight steps that any person who is with children at recess can undertake. Playworks has an online "recess checkup" system that can help to start this assessment.[10] I recommend a recess revitalization team composed of different stakeholders—perhaps including one or more administrators, a physical education or classroom teacher, the recess staff, and maybe even some students—who can work together to think about how to improve recess at school. Rethinking recess creates an opportunity to offer a leadership role to upper-grade students, who, with some adult support, can help with each of these steps.

STEP 1. **Assess the landscape.** What is the available space, and what are the fixed and moveable structures on it? Does the space have any safety hazards, such as places where children could trip and fall or where there are unsafe cracks in the pavement? Can these issues be fixed? Can garbage dumpsters or other hazards be moved away from where children play? (For more information on safety and school recess yards, see the US Consumer Product Safety Commission's report on playground safety.)[11] Where and what are the existing markings for games, if any? Where could markings be added? What other features of the space lend or detract from children's play?

STEP 2. **Assess the recess policies at school.** Is recess scheduled for every child every day? Do all teachers allow children to go to recess?

What are the rules regarding recess withholding for punishment or incomplete schoolwork? Can rules be instituted to ensure all children have recess time every day?

STEP 3. **Explore the play culture at school.** Are all children playing or engaged in some activity at recess? Can they start and sustain games or other play activities? What games do children of different age groups like to play? Could games that they might not already know or have the opportunity to play (such as four-square if markings were available or wall ball if the school has a good wall) be introduced? A number of resources are available for the kinds of recess games students like to play, if finding new games is of interest.[12]

STEP 4. **Engage in low-cost updates, if possible.** Sometimes low-cost updates can improve the recess experience tremendously. Adding new markings on blacktop or repaving, planting green spaces, removing hazards, or improving playground equipment can support an engaged recess climate. Many grants are available for efforts like these through local or national funders and corporate philanthropy (e.g., Nike, New Balance, Home Depot).[13]

STEP 5. **Provide necessary loose equipment, if possible.** Loose equipment such as balls and jump ropes can be the bane of school recess because, as many recess monitors report, the equipment is damaged or goes missing almost as soon as it arrives. Yet, it is essential to have the proper equipment for students to use so that they can play games during their break time. Schools can set up checkout systems for equipment like balls and jump ropes, and adults or students can be in charge of setting up cones or other markings for games, as well as taking them down at the end of recess. School parent-teacher associations often fund playground equipment, if such associations exist at the school and have funds to disburse. The same organizations that fund playground revitalization also fund loose equipment. Equipment used for PE class can be shared at recess, with some negotiation. Also, not all games require equipment. Games like "switch" (played on a four-square court), hopscotch, tag, relay races, and some traditional games like "mother may I" do not require any equipment at all. They may not be games children currently play, but if introduced, they could become play yard favorites.

STEP 6. **Centralize and systemize the equipment checkout.** If your school has precious little equipment, and pieces often go missing, the best way to protect it is to have students check it out from a ball cart or storage closet. The student who checks out the equipment is responsible for returning it to the same location and signing it back in. With a centralized system like this, students are aware of what equipment they have available to them, and adults can keep a closer eye on when equipment has gone missing in an effort to locate it. Centralizing equipment takes pressure off teachers to manage their class's equipment and encourages students to be responsible for the items they most like to use at recess.

STEP 7. **Map the play yard with different activity zones or game locations.** After steps 1–6 have been accomplished, it's time to map out the play yard. One goal is to ensure that the games children like most are available and that there is space for those who want to engage in their own imaginative play or have a quieter recess experience. A second goal is to create spaces that do not overlap so that jump rope does not spill over onto the basketball area, and students who play tag are not running through the soccer field during their game. To accomplish this in a small area, you may need to set up weekly rotations of games through the space. This rotation will also help to keep recess fresh for students. Based on play culture at the school, some core games may need to be available daily, but others could be rotated. Figures 3.1 and 3.2 provide sample play yard maps for large and small spaces, but these can and should be customized to the space, equipment available, and preferences of student players. The games may also need to be changed around for different age groups.

STEP 8. **Roll out the format to adults and students.** This may not be an "if you build it, they will come" kind of experience. To create a schoolwide emphasis on improving recess culture, schools need to take steps to inform the entire school community about the changes. First, the changes in recess format should be shared

FIGURE 3.1 Big play yard

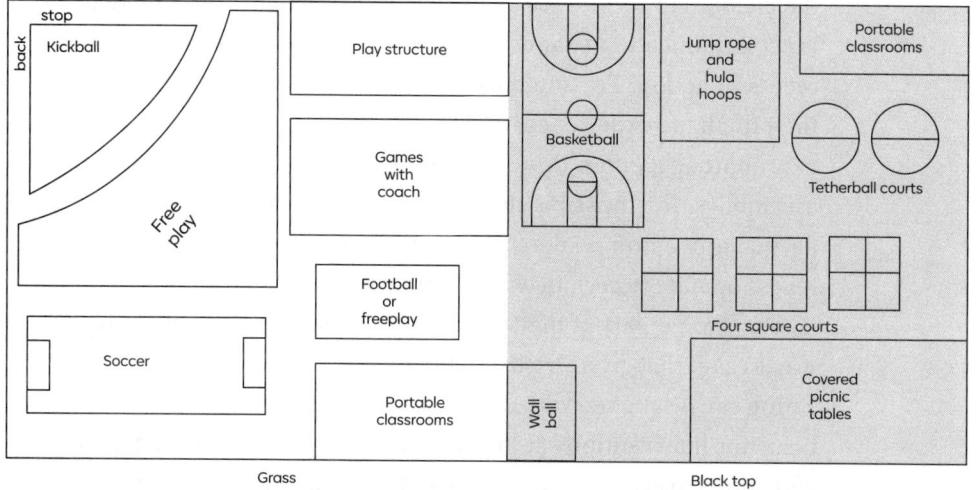

FIGURE 3.2 Small play yard

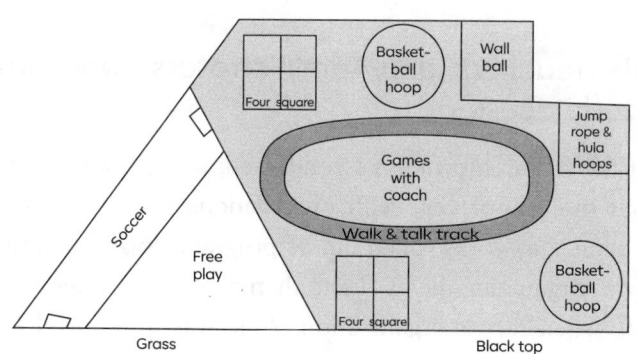

with teachers and other staff at school, both those who work at recess and those who do not. Students may have questions about the new recess format, and providing information to adults will be important for making sure consistent messages are shared. In addition, staff who monitor recess should be trained on the new format. All adults at recess should be aware of any new routines or game rules, and especially where certain games will be played.

Second, students and their families will also need to learn about the changes to recess. For families, this can happen through regular communication channels and invitations to come see the new recess in action. For students, changes can be presented through their firsthand experiences and also through an introduction to the new approach, either through classroom discussions or at student assemblies. It is possible that change will be met with resistance, particularly among older students who are accustomed to having recess operate in certain ways. Again, enlisting some of these older students to be part of the team that reorganizes recess might be a way to gain that group's trust in the process. If the recess reorganization can be aligned with other character development or positive behavior interventions at the school, this effort will help students and adults to see how important and necessary these changes are. This kind of intentional scaffolding is important, especially if the school does not have an existing culture of play.

Students, Teachers, and Administrators Appreciate Organized Recess

In one of the research projects I conducted, we followed recess change throughout the school year with observations and interviews at three points in time. Playworks rolled out its program slowly in these schools, starting with organizing the yard and then phasing in other components. In the fall, when recess organization alone was introduced to the play yard, students, teachers, and administrators were immediately sold on the approach. The initial organizational activities focused on three main changes: (1) mapping the play yard so that games had their own designated areas, (2) establishing common rules to games, and (3) creating equipment checkout stations.

When I first started working with the program and their leaders explained changes would be immediate as a result of their programming, I honestly did not believe them. I had been conducting implementation research on new programs for a number of years and knew that real change takes time. I was wrong; the changes described to us by school stakeholders happened quickly. For example, one principal felt this way after only six weeks of new recess organization at her school: "Just the feel as you walk around outside—it just feels different. The kids are involved.... I can see things getting organized." A teacher at the same school told us that organized recess allowed her students to play the game they most wanted: "It used to get chaotic. We had to stop soccer last year; kids were always getting hurt." With an organized approach and improved supervision, soccer was reinstated.

At another school, students also noticed a different feel at recess, even just a few weeks into the school year with the program. In a focus group of fourth- and fifth-grade students who had been chosen to help lead games at recess, one student told us this:

I know that there's more organized games, so that you don't just say, you don't say, "Hey, does anyone want to play dodgeball," 'cause usually people don't listen to you. But if it's an organized game, people actually do it, which is what I really like, and you actually have something to do.

Another student in the same focus group agreed and added her own thoughts, "There are a lot, lot more games, like there were barely any games last year." When I followed up to ask why there were more games, she responded, "They [students] know the rules to more games now." It was important to these students that games were not just located in predictable places, but that rules to the games were established so that all the children felt they could play.

Establishing common rules to games is a key to recess organization. In free play, children establish their own rules and negotiate, whereas in structured play, adults control the games and the rules. In organized recess, common rules to games are established, but they can be any set of rules to which children agree. There is not one right way to play a game. At one school working with their own recess staff and the program's advisors, a recess monitor discussed the pros and cons of common rules: "bringing those common rules, which is good and bad in some ways because there is some strength in having kids self-organize, but then there's also that danger of the hidden rules and the unfair play." Her point was that the common rules created a fairer play environment because rules were not arbitrary and could not be changed depending on who was in the game. With a predictable set of rules, all children can understand how the game operates and when it is their turn to play or not.

Agreeing to common rules can be among the more challenging pieces of organizing recess, especially if arbitrary game rules, which are unfair and discourage some children from having an opportunity to play, are an entrenched part of the recess culture at the school. For example, at one school my team visited, the four-square game had no fixed rules, but rather a culture that supported whoever was in the winning square to change the rules at their whim, playing to their own strengths rather than allowing others to have an equal chance of joining the game. When the recess team at this school attempted to change these rules to make them more objective, they faced student (and even parent) backlash, claiming that the new "fair" rules were ruining the four-square game. The assistant principal at the school described the situation like this:

> *I felt like there is a rationale for allowing kids to create rules and play along with those rules. Where the sweet spot is, though, is we don't want kids to become exclusive. That was also happening. The kinds of rules they had, it was like, how does the king ever, basically, once the king is in the king spot, then they made the rules up as they go.*

The school leadership opted to move slowly and created two four-square games—one with the new rules that would support an organized recess and the other with what they called old-school rules, basically the way things were before. The courts were labeled with chalk, and students could choose which game they preferred. As you might imagine, by the end of the school year, more students favored the fair rules, and the old-school game dwindled.

Schools posted their game rules in visible places near the spots where games were played. For instance, basketball rules written out on poster board and laminated were hung on a wall near the court, and sometimes posters were hung on equipment carts or sheds so students could see them as they checked out equipment. Posting game rules helps students to remember them and also to refer to them during a conflict so that they can fall back on what is established, and keep the game going, rather than argue about the rules and waste their play time. Early in the school year, a fifth-grade teacher at a school was reflecting on her experience the prior year and told us:

> *Before, we had all the equipment to play the games, but the kids never played them. I think I saw maybe one, maybe it's all different kids that would play four-square, and they didn't really know the rules. And there was often a lot of fighting because kids didn't know the rules. There was always, like, the pick-up soccer games, so there would end up being a lot of problems with those because there would be fighting in them. I think the biggest thing is that my kids would, a lot of them wouldn't participate in any game at all, that was the majority of kids. And so, we would see the kids bullying each other at recess because they didn't have anything else to do, so they'd walk around and do really mean things to each other.*

In this case, not having games with established rules discouraged students from playing and inadvertently—according to this teacher—led to behavioral problems. A first-grade teacher in another school explained that without rules, her students took games too far:

> *Well, the problem with first grade is they get very physical very fast. For example, last week I saw a few boys playing* Star Wars. . . . *Well, then they start, you know, shooting fake lasers at each other and light sabers, and then one decides just to progress and picks up grass and throws it at the other kid. Well, another one picks up sand and throws it, and pretty soon [I've] got boys that are wrestling on the ground, throwing sand in each other's eyes. . . . They really need that structure, those rules or, "Okay, this is what you do to play the game. If this happens, then you're out and you go to the back of the line," and, you know, they have a system to follow.*

This teacher was in favor of creative play but also wanted some organized activities so that her students could have positive experiences at recess and enjoy their time. She felt that without a common understanding of game rules, her students' playtime was not being used to its maximum potential and in fact devolved into conflict or disappointment.

In another school, a fourth-grade teacher felt that establishing common rules in organized games aided more creative play:

> *They are being more creative, I think, in their game play.... They would start playing this game, and I said, "What is this game?" "It's called 'chase the chicken'... we just made it up." And they were out there chasing this person, and I was like, "Oh, good, okay. Just don't knock each other down." Which they played really well. And I see a lot of integration between the boys and the girls.*

The rules I've been discussing pertain to specific games, but some schools also established rules related to all of recess. For instance, at one school a teacher explained that she teaches her students "Everyone can play because we're all friends," and this is a rule that the entire school follows at recess. Other recess rules might include "no pushing" or "only run in certain play yard locations."

Organization also helped to relieve pressure on teachers, who had previously been responsible for keeping track of the balls, jump ropes, or other loose equipment their students had available for recess. One teacher told us:

> *The equipment is one big difference. [Before] there wasn't a ball room. It was kept in individual classrooms and it got lost. There was a lot of arguing and conflict about jump ropes—who they belonged to and who could play/use them. This year there is some new equipment, and it's all been centralized to the equipment room. It's great because you, as a teacher, don't have to deal with it and everyone has ownership of it.*

Other teachers mentioned that having the equipment centrally managed had reduced conflict because students could see that the equipment belonged to everyone, not to just their classroom or just themselves. Centralizing equipment also provides an opportunity for students to learn how to be responsible for returning equipment and how to use it properly so that it does not break or get lost. If a ball is lost, that is everyone's ball, and students can see the effects at their next recess. Sometimes students are tempted to bring in their own balls or equipment to play with at recess, but doing so is generally discouraged in the schools I visited. One recess monitor explained:

> *Nobody's allowed to bring . . . their own balls and play equipment outside because we use the one for the whole school. So nobody says, "It's my ball; you're not allowed to play."*

Teachers and administrators, as well as support staff and others, view recess organization as an important piece of student engagement at recess. In a 2018 survey of nearly 5,500 teachers, administrators, and support staff members conducted by Playworks, half of respondents indicated that they felt the program significantly improved the number of students involved in healthy play. Among the 301 administrators who responded to the survey, 52 percent felt that there was a significant increase in recess engagement, including the variety of inclusive games.

Recess Needs Champions

What strategies can aid the process of recess organization? Ideally, each school would identify a recess revitalization team to help with the planning and a recess champion to spearhead the change efforts on the recess yard. The revitalization team should include a variety of stakeholders including administration, recess staff, teachers, counselors, and even students. Dividing steps 1 through 8 among a group of adults who are all committed to recess improvement and bring different skills to the effort is also a strong approach. Perhaps administrators focus on grant writing, and the physical education teacher focuses on game location on the play yard. The paraprofessionals or the school custodial staff can be responsible for identifying an equipment storage location, moving safety hazards, and painting new markings for games. Students can get involved with any or all of these activities, particularly in thinking about which games to locate where and what the common rules should be.

The recess champion leads the efforts day to day and can be any adult at the school, as long as administration is in agreement about the recess champion's role and that person is given time for the planning effort. In an ideal world, each school would have a recess coach to execute the recess organization plan. However, resource constraints may not allow for new staff, so many schools may need to tap into their existing staff's talents. Assistant principals, counselors, physical education teachers, or paraprofessionals can all be recess champions and be coaches who lead recess organization on the play yard if the administration is on board.

Regardless of the composition of the recess planning and implementation teams, the overall goal of their efforts is to make small yet powerful changes to recess organization that will be felt immediately. Once these changes become "the new normal," the school recess climate will adjust, and soon incoming students will never know there used to be a different way. Seeing and experiencing the rapid changes brought on by recess organization will give the school's student and adult stakeholders more faith and perhaps make them more open to more substantial changes that may be yet to come.

CHAPTER FOUR

Building a Culture of Play at Recess

Building a culture of play at recess that emphasizes having fun, feeling safe, and being healthy is a goal that most parents, teachers, administrators, and students can agree to, but how do we get there? Organizing the school yard in the ways discussed previously is an important first step. For administrators, teachers, and policy makers seeking to more deeply embed play into school culture and climate—because of its essential linkages to children's physical, social, emotional, and intellectual development—further steps can be taken. Adding elements to recess that support meaningful peer-to-peer and student-to-adult engagement, conflict resolution, and leadership opportunities as well as embedding play into school values can improve not only the recess climate but also the school climate throughout the day. These subtler elements can change the tone of recess in ways that encourage sustained play and inclusion, making it a more positive time for both students and adults.

The changes put in place from recess organization can be seen almost immediately. Within six weeks of organizing recess, adults at the schools my team visited expressed their positive views of how recess was flowing and the different ways that this change had positively affected student experiences. Making changes to embed a culture of play at recess is a longer-term objective, and although it can be accomplished in one school year when schools have strong leadership and vision, these are changes that schools might be expected to see over the longer term. Changing any organizational culture takes time, and schools are notoriously slow to adapt. With intention and leadership, embedding a culture of play at school is an achievable goal, and with it will come both anticipated and unexpected rewards.

At Northside Elementary, where Coach Diana had spent the year creating an organized recess environment and embedding a culture of play at recess, Principal Ramirez was sold on the approach. In a springtime interview, he talked about how the changes brought about by both recess organization and attention to culture of play changed his school for the better.

> *If you had an aerial shot of our school, the satellite photo, what you would have seen [in the past] would have been two huge, I mean huge, full, full soccer fields of grass completely . . . vacant, almost. So, maybe a few kids playing and a lot of kids on the blacktop, just kind of hovering about. But, whereas now, when you walk out at lunchtime, it's a lot of, I mean, both fields are taken up, and it's not kids fighting over . . . just because someone set up a goal here and goal there, that's the soccer field, so everyone has to fight over what they're doing, but, no, "We can easily set up another one over here." And a lot of sharing of the field. And a lot more spread out, where kids have different games spread out all over the field.*

Recess organization worked at this school. Principal Ramirez viewed the organization as successful because children were able to spread out and find places for their games, multiple games happened at once, and there was a lack of fighting over space, which was common before the organizational changes. Importantly, he also talked about how other aspects of building a culture of play took hold in the school year. For instance, he highlighted Coach Diana's way of helping children to see that fighting over a ball was wasting their valuable play time and that it is more important to play than to be right all the time.

> *Our teachers have actually taken Coach's lead on this . . . where she's taught the kids . . . if it's not a really serious issue, can you resolve it with [rock-paper-scissors]? You know, . . . "Yes, you've got the soccer ball, I wanted the soccer ball; I thought I should have it; you think you should have it." And they're done with it. Now, I've seen more and more teachers teaching the kids now that, where it's just simple, it's not a big deal, it's not the end of the world. "We're just going to very quickly decide who gets the ball now, and then I'll get it tomorrow."*

It is also important that Principal Ramirez saw the effects of introducing conflict resolution at recess on schoolwide practices. Many schools implement schoolwide behavioral or character development programs. It is important to align school values and expectations about behavior for times when children are in the classroom with values and expectations for recess time. These messages about positive behavior can be reinforced in the classroom when they are integrated at recess. However, achieving this goal may take time.

A teacher at this same school described two situations to us in a spring interview, the first where inclusion—a common theme in positive behavior and character development programs—was the new normal, and a second where students needed a reminder to play inclusively.

> *I have some really shy girls in this classroom that are . . . I see them out there, and I see them playing four-square or dodgeball. Much more. I think everyone is just feeling so much more comfortable with the games that they have and the toolbox of games that they have. And boys are asking girls to play, and girls are asking boys to play.*
>
> *And one of my kids came up to me the other day and said: "So-and-so said that I can't play. And I turned around to so-and-so, and I said, 'But that's not the way we play it. So, either we play by the rules, or I'm going to dismantle this game.' And she says, 'I'm sorry. No problem.'"*

Building a culture of play can help students who might be reluctant to move out of their comfort zone to play with their friends or others with whom they might not otherwise engage. Playing games or sports with other students, learning new skills, and building relationships with adults are all activities that can and should be fun for students at recess. Emphasizing play over winning as the primary goal of recess activities reduces pressure, increases inclusiveness, and helps students to see that their goal of recess is to play.

My research has led me to the conclusion that, although every school faces unique recess challenges, adults and students can implement a number of universally effective strategies to support a culture of play at recess and throughout the school day. Promoting a culture of play entails changing the tone of recess from one that is competitive and driven by conflict and "putting out fires" to one that is playful and fun. It also involves embedding school values into recess and recess values into the rest of the school day so the messaging and alignment between the two are consistent.

Seven specific strategies that I have observed promote a culture of play at recess, each of which is discussed in the sections that follow.

Requiring Recess for Every Child, Every Day

When a school takes steps to build a culture of play, it must signal to all teachers and students that all children deserve the right to recess every day at school. Children might not have recess every day for two reasons: (1) because it is not scheduled or the schedule is not always adhered to; and (2) because recess can be withheld from individual students or entire classes for behavioral problems or missed schoolwork. The first issue is relatively straightforward to address. When building the bell schedule, administrators should leave time for adequate breaks for children one or two times per day. These breaks should then be presented to teachers, lunch monitors, and other staff as mandatory parts of the day.

Changing school discipline policy and practice so that withholding recess is no longer a viable option is perhaps a more difficult goal. Withholding recess is a common punishment for students who are behind on their schoolwork or misbehave at recess and during other times of the day, even on the morning bus to school. On several occasions, we observed entire classes being held back from recess at the discretion of a recess or lunchroom supervisor, who may have no knowledge of extenuating circumstances that might lead students to be more rambunctious on a particular day. There is no evidence, however, that this is an effective strategy for eliciting improved behavior. If school leadership is committed to building a culture of play, maintaining each individual child's right to play at recess every day is essential.

> **Seven strategies to promote a culture of play**
>
> 1. Require recess for every child, every day.
> 2. Improve transitions to and from recess.
> 3. Promote inclusion and engagement.
> 4. Introduce simple conflict resolution strategies.
> 5. Encourage positive adult role models.
> 6. Establish student leadership at recess.
> 7. Plan for indoor recess.

What are alternatives to withholding recess? In my own research, I have seen few options because most schools continue to use that strategy for punishing children. Others have written about this issue, though, and offer some suggestions. Melinda Bossenmeyer at Peaceful Playgrounds has a toolkit of suggestions for alternatives to withholding recess.[1] She includes alternative punishments, such as having students write a letter to someone they may have hurt with their misbehavior or to their parents/guardians explaining why their behavior was inappropriate. She also suggests that students can lose a classroom privilege, such as having to make up schoolwork when other students have free time or to sit apart from the group and earn their way back into the class dynamic. The Center for Science in the Public Interest recommends detention before or after school and community service as alternatives to recess withholding.[2] Bossenmeyer and the Center for Science in the Public Interest both recommend incentivizing positive behavior with rewards rather than punishing negative behavior, such as extra recess time or choice in picking class activities, taking care of the class pet, or being the first to line up. Both also recommend working on classroom management techniques to help stop misbehavior before it can begin.

Principals have reported to me that often the same child over and over has recess withheld or ends up with a referral to the office for misbehavior.

In these cases, common classroom management strategies may be insufficient, and counselors or other resources may need to be brought in. However, even (or perhaps especially) these children deserve a time for recess every day. Children who have behavioral problems also need a break from the routine of the school day—a time to move their bodies or simply relax from the pressure of following directions in a structured environment. All children need breaks, and these breaks are especially important because they are students' main time to play at school and, as I've mentioned already, play is how children learn and grow—socially, emotionally, and physically. As the place where elementary-aged children spend the majority of their away-from-home time, school is an essential location for play to occur, and preserving the right to play for every child during the school day should be a priority.

Improving Transitions to and from Recess

Transitions can be difficult for children, so creating transition routines that support their play, rather than detract from it, can help children to make the most of their recess time. Students generally arrive at recess from either their classroom or from the lunchroom. Sometimes an adult walks them to recess, and other times the outside doors open and they run out unaccompanied. In some schools—mainly on the East Coast in my research—students are asked to line up when they arrive at recess and are then released when a recess monitor or coach feels they are calm enough to begin recess. In other schools, no lining up is required. At Playworks schools, the coach generally checks in with students as they come to recess, reminding them of the game offerings before they run off to play. There is no one right way to transition children to recess, but some strategies can be employed to help the transition process.

First, adults who are responsible for recess monitoring should temper their expectations about students' abilities to stand still and quiet while waiting for what seems like an excruciatingly long time to be released to recess. I have observed recess monitors walking up and down lines of young children admonishing even the slightest movement and keeping an entire class from playing because of one child who simply cannot stand still. This is usually done in the name of safety, to keep children from pushing in line. However, children can move without pushing, so this practice of requiring stillness is, in my experience, pointless. Schools provide recess so that children can have a time to move, and requiring military-like precision of eight-year-olds waiting to run free is unnecessary. Holding students back from play until they can stand still also reduces the limited time students have for a break and negatively affects students' relationships with adult monitors at recess.

Instead of requiring stillness of students waiting to go to recess, monitors and coaches who have information to relay to students about recess can require attention. Students can pay attention to instructions even if they are not in perfectly straight lines. Another technique I have observed is to have a call-and-response clap to get attention or a whistle to give a brief set of instructions and then release students. If multiple classes or grades are at recess together, these techniques can be used all at once or class by class as students arrive at recess.

The transition back to class at the end of recess can be the more challenging one. Again, I have observed monitors who require children to stand perfectly still and be quiet, and who will yell at and admonish them to behave if they are not able to do this. Lining up at the end of recess is practical for many reasons, including that getting in line makes it much easier for a teacher who is picking up students to find them all in one place and lead them quietly through the halls back to their classroom. Some other strategies can help students to calm themselves after play and shift their mindset back into school mode.

In most schools bells ring at the start or end of periods, and these bells often demarcate the end of recess for students. With multiple grades or classes arriving and leaving recess at different times, these bells can ring multiple times during any given recess period, which can be confusing for students. Simplifying the bell schedule is one way to ease transitions. It is much easier for children to leave recess when all of them are leaving together. Still, having a hundred or more children leave the recess yard (especially a small one) at once can create chaos. One effective strategy is that when the bell rings, the coach blows a whistle and children must stop their play and take a knee, just for a few seconds. Then the coach again blows the whistle and children must return their equipment and walk back to the doors where they return to class. Having everyone on the play yard stop at once creates a collective transition moment that children can easily see ends recess and begins their movement back to class. Of course, there are always stragglers, but having one common process for ending recess helps even these students to make the transition back.

Once students return to the school doors, what happens next depends on how teachers pick up their students or if students are going to lunch after they play. Students going directly to lunch can stop at a handwashing station and head into their cafeteria or eating area. For those going to class, existing school processes may dictate the next steps. In some schools, students line up in specific places, and their teachers come to meet them and take them back to class. In other schools, students are herded by paraprofessionals. Sometimes students are kept waiting for an adult escort, which can lead to undesirable behavior (pushing and shoving in line, for instance). Employing some distraction techniques during this time can be helpful, if necessary, teaching children call-and-response claps or chants, which can also serve to help them build school spirit if these responses involve something having to do with the school mascot. There is no magic to these activities; they are simply distractions and entertainment so that children have something to do while waiting and build rapport with the adult coach. Still, minimizing the wait time is the best way to ease the transition back to class or lunch.

Promoting Inclusion and Engagement

Building a culture of play at recess requires a mindset shift from a competitive play yard, where winning is the goal and exclusive play the norm, to one where sustained play is valued over winning and inclusion is the goal. This change is among the most difficult to make at recess because competition is fiercely valued and promoted in US society, even (or especially) in schools. Children are accustomed to gleefully yelling "you're out" and doing the equivalent of touchdown dances when they score a point or a goal, often to the dismay or shame of their opponent. In the next moment, the tides could turn. Is this kind of behavior really a necessary part of school yard play? I argue that it is counterproductive to a safe and healthy recess. Competition has its place, but school recess should be a space where children have the opportunity to join any game, to feel safe while playing, and to try new activities so they can develop physical, social, and emotional skills.

Building on the work that has already been done to organize recess, the adults who supervise children at recess now have the opportunity to change the recess climate by modeling the goals and values of a culture of play. Whether it's led by a recess coach, a team of supervisors, or a physical education teacher, actively promoting recess engagement and enjoyment is part of creating a culture of play at recess. To improve engagement and enjoyment at recess requires two main changes: (1) changing the culture of the recess yard from one that allows exclusive and competitive games to one that encourages all students to be included in any game and (2) creating a supportive environment that makes being out just part of the game and encourages students to applaud, rather than denigrate, each other during play.

In the most competitive games at a school—typically boys' soccer or basketball—students are deeply invested in their game, often play together every day, typically get a fair amount of physical activity, and can often keep their game going during recess. However, these games are also exclusive, available only to students who are invited, and typically exclude others who want to play but are not perceived as being good enough players to join. These games can also be contentious and devolve into physical fights at the height of competitive play. How does a school deescalate its most competitive games and make them inclusive? There are several strategies. One is to add another court or field of an uber-competitive game that is inclusive and not competitive. This approach allows a well-running competitive game to continue and creates another opportunity to cater to other students. The less competitive game could be a different version; for example, Playworks has versions called three-line soccer or knockout basketball that offer a way to rotate more children on and off the court.[3]

However, sometimes the very competitive games are not productive times even for those who are the best athletes, and instead participants end up arguing or fighting, feelings are hurt, and students end recess not feeling satisfied with their time. In this case, administrators might choose to shut

> **Three-line soccer rules to be posted on the play yard**
>
> - Three lines, three players per team.
> - Rock-paper-scissors to go first.
> - First team to score stays in.

down the uber-competitive game for a short while and then reopen it with an adult present to help organize teams and support play. The new game would have a common set of rules and someone to help teach children these rules while supporting their continued play. This technique may sound simple, but as many educators and parents know, it is not. Students who are accustomed to unfettered soccer will be frustrated or angry; they or their parents may complain or even go to the local media. Communication with students and parents about the plans for the game is important if a beloved, yet fraught, game is to be shuttered for a time or reorganized.

Changing the way games are played, with the goal being sustaining play rather than winning, is a related strategy. For instance, in a game like tetherball where only two students can play at a time, how can the other children remain engaged while waiting for their turn? The game can be altered so that it moves quickly and students have more chances to play. For instance, instead of the winning player occupying the court permanently, that person gets three chances to be the winning player and then must go to the end of the line. While students wait in line, they can be encouraged to cheer for the other players whether they win or lose. Using encouraging language like "good job, nice try" or giving a high five to a student who gets out, thus normalizing the process of losing a turn and offering support rather than shaming a person for simply moving through the game, is another strategy. Adult modeling is the key for changing play yard vernacular in this way. When children see an adult who lost at tetherball walk down the line of observers giving and receiving high fives and not feel shame (or experience jeers), this behavior helps them to understand how to exhibit good sportsmanship.

A question is how should these changes should be communicated to students: should recess supervisors simply start acting differently, or should students and parents receive messaging in advance of the changes?

Strong communication between school and home is essential for building a positive learning environment and supporting school climate, and I recommend being up front with all stakeholders about changes to recess. Messaging about the alignment between recess time and behavior supports or character development programs is one way to put a positive spin on the new changes and to encourage teachers, as well as recess monitors, to be part of the process.

Introducing Conflict Resolution Strategies

Conflict is a normal part of play. In games where children are invested and engaged, we should expect there to be disagreements about whether a ball is in or out, who goes first, who is on which team, if someone was tagged properly or not, and so on. Being able to resolve these conflicts quickly and continue to play is a key learning opportunity for children at recess. Schools approach conflict resolution on the recess yard in different ways. Some schools encourage children to seek out an adult for all conflicts, small or large. Others encourage a talk-it-out approach, with adult intervention as a backup if that fails. I've been to schools where there is no communication about or approach to resolving recess conflicts and students are left to figure that out on their own. I've also been to schools where every conflict that is not resolved by students results in a referral to the principal. In many schools my team visited, teachers told us that they use a variety of student behavior management techniques, including conflict resolution, in their classrooms, but that these techniques do not carry over onto the recess yard. The reason is that recess is often overlooked as a place for creating a positive school climate. Teachers and others who might be tasked with school climate improvement efforts are often not recess supervisors, and the adults who do supervise recess are typically not included in trainings or professional development offered to educators. This mismatch can be corrected to ensure consistent messaging about behavior and school expectations.

Changing the play culture so that keeping the game going is the main goal is an important aspect of building a culture of play. Introducing a simple conflict resolution tool at recess to support continued play and deescalate

> **Alternative ways to play rock-paper-scissors**
>
> - Play with your feet! Rock = feet together. Paper = feet spread out to sides. Scissors = feet spread front and back.
> - Play with the whole body! Rock = body curled up. Paper = standing straight arms to sides. Scissors = arms high and wide, legs out wide.

competition can quickly resolve many recess problems so that children can sustain their games. The tool employed by Playworks is the game rock-paper-scissors. In this game, students use one hand to indicate a rock, paper, or a scissor; paper beats rock, rock beats scissors, scissors beats paper. There are many variations to this game with different icons, but the basic idea is that each child picks one icon and who wins is determined by the icons selected.[4] It is random. What makes this tool work at recess is that it can be used quickly on the spot and without adult intervention so that the game play can proceed. A common pitfall to avoid is turning rock-paper-scissors into a two-out-of-three competition (which is often the inclination of the losing party). Schoolwide agreements that you use rock-paper-scissors one time and everyone agrees to the outcome are important. Because the outcome is random, students will understand and experience that they can be on the losing side one day or in one moment but win the next time.

When rock-paper-scissors is deployed successfully at recess, teachers report they also see students using it in the classroom to make teams or decide who goes first in a group activity. They may not have thought of this simple game as a way to manage classroom behavior, but teachers report that it works well with their existing class management techniques and can be easily integrated into everyday practices.

Although rock-paper-scissors is an easy-to-use conflict resolution tool, not all recess conflicts can be easily resolved. For instance, exclusion is a common problem on elementary play yards, and students cannot rock-paper-scissors their way out of feeling excluded by classmates. Bullying is another problem that is not quickly or easily resolved with simple conflict resolution tools. These deeper problems require adult guidance and intervention, modeling, and sometimes one-on-one support or even parental intervention. When schools set up a play yard that builds a culture of play, the recess climate can support more inclusion and minimize common play yard problems to help adults focus their attention where it is most needed.

There will always be a few students at recess for whom even the most well-thought-out conflict resolution strategies will not work. Students with social or emotional developmental needs that make it difficult for them to follow rules or behave appropriately at recess will likely not respond as well to these strategies. Principals have told me that, for whatever reason, some students just seek out trouble. In the absence of recess engagement, these students can encourage their peers to spend their recess time in nonproductive ways that lead to misbehavior among more students. With conflict resolution and other engagement tactics in place, however, students who have tendencies to bully or get in trouble may have a less available audience for their antics, or they may have found something more productive to do. With recess engagement and simple conflict resolution tools to keep the game going, many students will be busier and less susceptible to negative influence.

There will always be conflicts at recess that require adult intervention, and having a plan for these more serious episodes is important. Alignment with schoolwide behavior expectations can help students to understand why certain behaviors have consequences. For instance, if a school focuses on compassion as part of a character development program, children should be taught what that looks like specifically at recess: compassion means that anyone can play, or compassion means that students use encouraging words to cheer on others even if they are waiting their turn to play. Changing the tone of recess from one that is competitive and conflict-driven to one that is playful and fun is also a major part of conflict resolution.

Encouraging Positive Adult Role Models

Children are excited when adults play with them, and my recess observations indicate that when an adult is playing at recess, children flock to that game. By organizing the play yard, encouraging children, and participating in their games, adults have the opportunity to become recess-time role models. Adults are the ones who set the tone for recess. Adults who are playful and engage with students demonstrate a positive tone that recess is a time for fun and signal their interest in connecting with children. Those who stand off to the side and ignore children while talking to colleagues, or who yell at children when they intentionally or inadvertently break the rules, demonstrate a more negative tone for recess and signal that they are not approachable. Adults who supervise recess should model the language and behavior they want to see in children and explain to children why they want to do these things.

Building relationships between children and adults is a key part of positive school climate, and recess is one of the only periods during the day when adults have the time to get to know children in an uncontrolled environment. Sometimes the recess staff are the only school personnel who see every single child every single day. They have the chance to be a positive influence in that child's life but do not always see this as their role. When adult recess monitors choose to ignore children or behave negatively toward them during recess, the school also misses an important opportunity to support growth in children's social, emotional, and physical development.

Recess monitors or coaches who are positive adult role models engage in three types of activities: they play with children, they actively support children's play, and they model inclusive behavior and positive messaging at recess. Children want to play with adults and especially the adults at school. Plan a teachers versus students kickball game and you'll see what I mean. Adults who play at recess often have a following of students who will play whatever game they start. At nearly every Playworks school my team visited, the students, teachers, and principal would refer to the coach as a "rock star," using that exact phrase, describing the ways that children respect and idolize their coaches and want to be part of any game they are playing. Any adult can be a rock star at recess. Playing with children allows children to see that adults are approachable, demonstrates the value the school places on play, allows adults to connect and build relationships with students, and especially creates opportunities for adults to engage in a positive way with students who may have trouble controlling their behavior at recess. Engaging in play also provides an opportunity for adults to model what it looks like to follow the rules, resolve simple conflicts, take their turn in the game, and win and lose gracefully.

Not all adults want to play or are physically capable of playing, but they can support recess in other ways. Adults can also support play by standing on the sidelines as engaged and neutral fans, cheering for students, ensuring fair play and rule following, helping students to be included, and becoming involved through less active engagement including turning jump ropes, helping to organize teams, and the like. Being a play supporter generates some of the same positive relationship building and culture of play building outcomes as actually playing with children.

When asked what their role is, recess monitors nearly universally say their primary role is to keep children safe. However, there are many ways to keep children safe, and admonishing them to follow rules is only one such way. Schools can also support adults who are monitoring recess to change their own recess behaviors to model what healthy interactions look like. Adults should adhere to the same code of conduct as students during recess—for example, using positive language, treating others with respect, and being inclusive.

Maintaining adequate coverage so that adults can both ensure student safety and have an opportunity to engage with students is important. Relying on teachers or administrators for coverage is often problematic because they have competing priorities; they may be called away for a district meeting or to handle a crisis with a student. Hiring a coach or designating one recess monitor to be the acting recess coach is a particularly good strategy for ensuring that culture of play is established while maintaining safety at recess. Partnering with local agencies such as the Parks and Recreation department, a youth or teen center, or the local Boys & Girls Club or YMCA is another way to try to recruit recess-time help. These agencies often run afterschool programs and may have staff members who are available during the school day to play with students at recess and lead games that they might not otherwise play. I observed this kind of partnership in several middle schools I visited recently. Although the volunteers were not integrated into the school supervision team in any way, their games did draw in students who were not otherwise engaged into play, and the volunteers themselves seemed to be well liked by students and adults.

Having enough adults at recess to ensure children are safe and adults can engage with children in their play is critical for establishing the culture of play at recess.

Establishing Student Leadership at Recess

Making changes to the tone of recess and the culture of play does not need to be solely the purview of the adults in a school. Students can also have a major role in promoting recess through leadership opportunities. Indeed, offering opportunities for students to be involved in school climate change is an important way to both garner student buy-in for changes that are introduced and also to provide opportunities for social and emotional development to students who might not otherwise have the chance.

There are few examples of elementary school leadership programs, but one that stands out is Playworks' junior coach program. Junior coaches are typically fourth- and fifth-grade students, perhaps twenty per year, who are trained by and work closely with recess coaches to lead games at their own recesses and, if schedules allow, the recesses of younger children. They spend time learning the game and recess rules, how to help students to resolve conflicts, how to model inclusive behavior and positive language, and what their own behavior should be like at recess.

Are ten- and eleven-year olds really capable of leading games at recess? Yes! I have observed a number of recess periods where there was an ineffective recess coach or none at all and where older elementary students in purple junior coach T-shirts were the ones to run recess and support younger students to play. In the many junior coach focus groups my team has conducted, the resounding message we have gathered is that students themselves truly enjoy this role in part because they have the opportunity to connect with other students with whom they might not normally engage.

Selecting who should be a recess leader is an important task. It would undermine the leadership opportunities at the school to take only those students who are already leaders in the classroom—the top-performing and most well-behaved students at school—although having a few of them is a good idea. It's also a good idea to promote students who already exhibit leadership qualities at recess, those students who are very athletic, well liked by their peers, or outgoing. Including as leaders a few students who have tendencies to misbehave at recess can be a strategy to help to turn around their behavior. More than one teacher has told me that she uses the junior coach status of her students to remind them about their own behavior and status as a role model when they are off duty.

> **Junior coach roles**
>
> - Set up recess yard with cones or other equipment.
> - Disburse equipment, like balls.
> - Support a game by playing with students and helping to resolve conflicts.
> - Model inclusive behavior.
> - Model good sportsmanship.

Scheduling for junior coaches to be available during younger students' recess periods and training them to perform their duties require a strong commitment on the part of school administration to emphasize this leadership opportunity and encourage students, teachers, and recess supervisors to participate. Resources may also be required so that recess supervisors can be paid to engage with junior coaches before or after school for training and meetings. These costs or scheduling constraints may prove to be prohibitive, but there are other models for incorporating student leadership.

Even if students cannot be available for younger students' recess periods, they can still be junior leaders at their own recesses and not have to miss any academic instruction time. They can also play a less active role, and instead of running games, they can start by managing the equipment, setting up the games with cones or other markings, giving the instructions for what games are available on a particular day, or performing any number of other organizational tasks that can build their connection to recess and demonstrate that student input is valued at school.

Many schools, particularly middle and high schools, have student government or leadership teams composed of student officers who make policy recommendations and organize events on campus. These activities are typically overseen by a teacher or administrator. The same kind of leadership opportunity could be made available to elementary students, with a focus on recess or school climate. This student school climate task force could work with school leadership to help with the steps for organizing recess. They could also poll their classmates about their favorite games and how they would like to see recess improved, be involved with painting markings on blacktop or cleaning the recess yard as a community event, and participate in the process in other appropriate ways. Even if students do not have an ongoing role in helping to make recess run more smoothly, encouraging student involvement in planning and execution may lead to more student investment in the recess improvement process and allow students to gain leadership skills, such as public speaking, organization, and listening to others.

Planning for Indoor Recess

What happens to recess when it is moved indoors either temporarily in milder climates when it rains or for months on end in colder climates? Having a well-organized recess that promotes a culture of play on the outdoor play yard can aid tremendously efforts to engage students in indoor recess as well.

Many factors go into what happens on indoor recess days, including indoor space availability and location, teachers' contractual agreements for breaks and their desire to keep their rooms open for students, and whether a cafeteria is available for lunch, among others. Needless to say, indoor recess does not offer the same opportunities for engagement in play as outdoor recess, but when students do spend their time indoors, how can a culture of play guide their activities?

The best-case scenario for indoor recess is that the same offerings available outdoors could also be available indoors. With some creativity, schools have turned their gym or a multiuse room into a play space that allows for a variety of games using temporary markings like masking tape or cones. Two problems get in the way of this solution. First, not all schools have a large gymnasium or multiuse room. Second, sometimes schools that have these spaces are using them for other activities, such as physical education class or lunch, during the time that other classes have recess, so they are unavailable.

What are alternative options? Adults will need to find spaces that can be repurposed for play during recess time. Classrooms with desks can be reorganized so that games can be played. Running games like soccer and basketball may not be on offer, but other games can still be a source of fun. For example, there are hide-and-seek games, "statue" or "freeze" games (where students must stand still in one position), games that use the four corners of a classroom for sorting and re-sorting students, games that use rock-paper-scissors as a basis for moving up or being out, and so on. Yoga or stretching, web-based movement programs, games with balloons or foam balls, and many other opportunities exist for an engaged and at least somewhat active indoor space. Many resources for these activities are available online, and it is not my goal to detail the many options but merely to say that play can happen indoors and inside a classroom, when weather requires.

My research has been focused mainly on outdoor recess yard activities, but weather is unpredictable and every so often my team also observed indoor recess. This was the case at one East Coast school I visited. On a rainy day in the spring, I learned that teachers took their own lunch break during recess and were not available to supervise students in classrooms. The gym at this school was being used for physical education class during recess. For years, students had been kept inside in the cafeteria in inclement weather, sitting at long tables for their entire break, instead of having time to eat and time to play as they did when there was outdoor recess. Behavior at these cafeteria-bound recesses was reportedly highly problematic. When Playworks came into this school, the coach searched widely for an alternative space to move at least some of the students so they could play at recess. She landed in an antiquated auditorium with a large stage and ancient-looking theater-style seats that were fixed in their spots. The space was far from ideal, but the coach designed it so that two classes of thirty students could occupy the auditorium safely at once. Several games of four-square were marked off, and a space for jump rope and other contained games was located on the stage. The three aisles of the auditorium were used for races of different kinds. Not all classes could be in the space at once, so they rotated which ones had their day in the auditorium and which stayed in the cafeteria. With fewer students in the cafeteria, those who remained had more space to spread out and engage in activities as well. The school did not do this, but the cafeteria space could have been used to have students engage in quiet movement activities or even games like "mother may I" or musical chairs, if an adult had been willing, trained, and available to organize these activities.

Based on the limited indoor recess observations I have gathered, that is precisely what I predict would happen with an embedded culture of play. Over time, if leadership supports a culture of play and recess supervisors are supported to learn how to engage differently with children, when teachers see the value of play for their students and students realize that playing is more fun than standing around or fighting, indoor recess can become playful and engaging.

Overcoming Challenges and Resistance to Change

The two biggest challenges I have heard about in my research on recess transformation are resources and time. Both are limited in schools, especially low-income urban schools, and either can delay or derail even the most well-thought-out reform efforts. I have no magic words on these fronts but do have some suggestions on how to pursue resources. Schools I have visited have used their Title I funds to support recess reform and have tied recess changes to initiatives on social and emotional learning, physical education and activity, or school climate. They have capitalized on the focus of school district committees or initiatives to ask for (and sometimes receive) additional funds to support more staff or equipment at recess. The arguments I have presented in this book make a strong case that, if left unattended, recess can be linked to everything from childhood obesity to the school-to-prison pipeline, and these arguments can be used to implore district committees to consider recess funding. This effort does take time and possibly resources, as well as a champion at the school. One possible way to gain extra support is to recognize this and seek alignment with other school and district commitments to share resources. If fundraising is a possibility in your community, communicating school goals for recess and what it would take to get there could be an opportunity to seek donations or sponsorships from local businesses to help the effort.

Some adults, no matter how much they like children, do not want to play physical games with them. School staff are overwhelmingly women, some of whom may not feel confident in their athletic skills, may have health limitations, or may prefer to wear clothing and footwear that are not conducive to play yard games. They may remember their own experiences at recess or in physical education class as something less than happy, and they may be reluctant to get involved. Overcoming this resistance is important. Not all recess supervisors need to play, but as I pointed out in the section on adult roles, all adults can support play even if they never actively participate in games. However, finding those people at school who will play with students is essential, and as recess staff turn over, adding playing with children to job descriptions for recess supervisors and providing training on what that means are ways to make these changes over time.

Never have I been to a school where leadership is simply uninterested in improving recess, but I have been to schools where teachers and recess supervisors resist changes to recess, either because these changes are perceived as creating more work for them, or because new role designations to support a culture of play create hard feelings or confusion among other staff members. In one school I visited, a recess supervisor was promoted to recess coach and offered new responsibilities for organizing and leading the play yard. She worked closely with administrators during the year but met ongoing resistance from the physical education teacher, who volunteered at recess most days and felt he was better qualified for this role. Because supervising recess was not formally part of his duties, he was not eligible for the position. Although his opinion was sought and participation encouraged, he actively attempted to derail the recess coach's attempts to make improvements during the year, even when it was clear that children were responding positively to the changes. However, during the course of the year, his resistance to change morphed from an overall disapproval to focusing in on one aspect of the play yard—the distractions the coach used when lining up students. His derision about her call-and-response techniques was annoying to the recess coach, but she felt her victories had overshadowed his protests during the course of the year.

I have also visited schools in which teachers never supervise recess and take no interest in what's happening during that time. In schools that had seen what I would characterize as a major transformation in how recess operated, my team interviewed teachers that knew almost nothing about what was happening during that time. Integrating teachers in recess transformation, including teachers who express opposition, is important for building a culture of play at school. They may not be the experts or the implementers, but teachers are an important stakeholder group and are very knowledgeable about their own students' needs and challenges. Building a culture of play also requires strong administrative leadership and investment from the entire school community. Making it a whole school change will encourage teachers, even the least interested in recess, to incorporate some of the changes embedded in a culture of play—conflict resolution, inclusive and positive behavior—into the classroom. This is a key way for these reforms to make an even larger difference at school.

Aligning School and Recess Values with a Culture of Play

Although this culture of play might originate at recess, other aspects of the school day can feed into or benefit from adopting this approach. For instance, a strong alignment between physical education and recess can promote improved experiences for children in both contexts. Some schools use a strategy called "class game time" for the recess coach to teach games to individual classes of students that they can play at recess. However, these same games can be taught and practiced in physical education class. Learning games in a more structured setting allows students to master the skills and understand the rules they need to play. Then they will feel more prepared to play those games with other students at recess.

Many schools choose to integrate their recess priorities with other school behavior or character development programs. We visited many schools that were implementing Positive Behavioral Intervention and Supports, a program that rewards positive behaviors and supports social and emotional skill building. Other schools we visited had character development programs or slogans, such as "the five *B*s: Being responsible, being safe, being cooperative, being respectful, and being prepared," or ROAR, which stands for "respect, ownership, aspire and reflect." Another used the motto "be respectful, be responsible, make good choices," and yet another incorporated the rules "be safe, be respectful, be responsible." All these school maxims were noted on banners and included part of school climate-boosting strategies, and each can be integrated into the recess environment and aligned with a culture of play to make meaningful reforms at recess.

The key is to get the whole school community to view recess as an integral part of the school day and one that supports all the school's goals, including student achievement. This emphasis includes messaging to school staff, parents, district leaders, and students that play is how children learn and we should value play for its physical activity and opportunities for social and emotional skill building. Alignment with school values and behavioral programs is essential, and empowering students to have leadership in their recess and encouraging adults to play with or actively engage with students at recess are important ways to develop a positive recess climate. This positive recess climate, in turn, will support student learning of essential social and emotional skills, reduce time spent on conflict resolution and discipline, and build a culture of play at school.

CHAPTER FIVE

Social and Emotional Learning Thrives at Recess

Social and emotional competence is the ability to understand, manage, and express the social and emotional aspects of one's life in ways that enable the successful management of life tasks such as learning, forming relationships, solving everyday problems, and adapting to the complex demands of growth and development. It includes self-awareness, control of impulsivity, working cooperatively, and caring about oneself and others.[1]

Culligan Elementary School is one of only a few schools in a suburban district that serves a majority of low-income and English learning students. In the year I visited, Culligan was implementing a recess reform effort that was supported by Playworks but driven and overseen by school personnel. The reforms were aimed at making recess a more fun and less conflict-ridden space for children, but these efforts had reverberating effects that could be seen both at recess and back in the classroom.

Fifth-grade teacher Ms. Griggs, who had the opportunity to observe recess reforms firsthand, felt they were successful:

> *I think it's made things a lot more calm out on the playground. It's teaching a lot more kids how to interact with each other and how to be more inclusive rather than exclusive. I think that's been the big benefit because in the past there's always been kids saying, "Well, I can't play. They won't let me play," and now they're more welcoming of others to play. They know the rules, so there's not the fighting over what's supposed to be going on.*

Ms. Griggs was pleasantly surprised to see how this newfound collegiality crossed over from recess into her classroom. For instance, she felt her students came back from recess calmer, more ready to learn, and better able to collaborate. Reflecting on this behavior, she said, "Yes, the academics are important, but elementary school is really learning how to get along with others, how to work with others, how to cooperate." Ms. Griggs also had several students who were junior coaches, selected to help work at their own and younger students' recess periods to support safe and healthy play. Her junior coaches used their training to help on indoor recess days, and she said, "They're getting involved with their fellow students and ... giving them ideas of things they can do other than run around and chase each other in the classroom."

These descriptions offered by Ms. Griggs are examples of students transferring the social and emotional learning that happened at recess back to her classroom. She observed a positive change in how her students interacted with each other, and she felt this difference was incredibly important because, to her, acquiring and solidifying social and emotional skills are key for elementary students before they move on to middle school.

Today, educators and policy makers are focused on social and emotional learning as a way to promote academic achievement and student success. The US Department of Education's National Center on Safe Supportive Learning Environments highlights social and emotional learning practices; on its website are research, technical assistance, and many examples of how educational environments can help support social and emotional learning for students of all ages. Thousands of schools nationwide are implementing curricula aimed at building students' social and emotional skills using a variety of strategies. A 2017 publication documented eleven states nationwide that have adopted goals and benchmarks for elementary-aged students' development in social and emotional competencies and noted that many more local districts and schools are similarly moving in this direction.[2] Social and emotional learning is a strategy that can be universally applied in education reform because all children—from the youngest to the oldest, across ethnic and socioeconomic groups—must develop social and emotional skills to be successful in twenty-first-century workplaces and in their adult lives.[3] Promoting social and emotional skills is also thought to be a key to prevention because acquisition of these skills is a necessary condition for the success of many of the existing prevention programs (e.g., suicide, teen pregnancy, substance abuse, and violence).[4] Strong consensus exists among educators and the public that schools should be teaching a range of competencies to students, including goal setting, communication skills, collaboration, and character—taking a "whole child" approach to education.[5]

Where does recess fit in to the social and emotional learning process? Recess is a place that children can both learn and practice social and emotional skills. The organizational and supportive practices described previously double as practices to promote social and emotional learning. However, established social and emotional learning programs focus mainly on classroom experiences and teacher interactions. These are obviously critically important contexts, but they are also more structured and offer less time for natural peer interactions where social and emotional skills can be practiced. As a less structured learning environment, recess also is a time when children can build and practice their social and emotional skills, but it is often overlooked as a space for teaching them. In this chapter, I argue that recess is an essential time in the day to support this kind of learning.

What exactly are the social and emotional skills that prepare elementary students for their healthy and productive future lives? The Collaborative for Academic, Social, and Emotional Learning (CASEL)—widely known and respected as the organization in the forefront of research and programming in this area—describes the five key social and emotional

> **CASEL's five key social and emotional skills for elementary-aged children**
>
> - *Self-awareness*: identifying one's own feelings and recognizing how they affect others.
> - *Self-management*: regulating emotions and behaviors, including controlling impulses and persisting in challenging situations.
> - *Social awareness*: understanding social norms for behavior and empathizing with others, particularly those whose cultural or ethnic backgrounds may not match one's own.
> - *Relationship skills*: establishing and maintaining relationships with different kinds of people, including communicating clearly, negotiating conflict, and seeking help.
> - *Responsible decision-making*: making good choices about personal behavior and social interactions.

skills for elementary-aged children: self-awareness, self-management, social awareness, relationship skills, and responsible decision-making.[6]

Social and emotional learning (SEL), the process through which these skills are acquired, is an important part of elementary education, and these skills can be taught to students through a variety of implicit and explicit learning strategies. Researchers at CASEL conducted a review of SEL programs and found that they generally integrated two sets of strategies.[7] First is instruction in "processing, integrating and selectively applying social and emotional skills" in ways that are appropriate for students given their developmental stage and cultural or community context.[8] Importantly, this strategy includes (for teachers) teaching and modeling skills and (for students) having the opportunity to practice these skills. The second set of strategies involves establishing safe and caring learning environments, including both classroom-based contexts and whole-school initiatives. In other words, for classroom-based SEL programs to take hold, both classroom and other school environments (like recess!) must also provide support for SEL.

These two strategies can be employed in explicit SEL programs or by focusing more on implicit learning through everyday lessons.[9] The more explicit SEL programs use curricula and specific lesson plans that are deployed outside the regular academic curricula to teach students—usually in a classroom setting—to label, support, and use social and emotional skills. Implicit approaches instead integrate SEL into the regular academic curricula by incorporating it, for instance, into lessons on reading and comprehension or by providing capacity building to teachers on how to interact with students to facilitate students' SEL.

In both cases, having an opportunity to practice social and emotional skills in a real-world setting, such as at recess, is essential for solidifying this learning.[10] Indeed, one of the main reasons why SEL programming can fail to elicit its intended results is that the SEL intervention is not fully adopted, missing key opportunities for skill building.[11] To support SEL programs, recess, like other parts of the school day, should embed opportunities for practicing these skills.

For the many schools that do not operate any SEL programming, recess is even more important because implementing practices to intentionally scaffold social and emotional learning during this time can help students to learn these skills in a safe environment. In well-executed recess periods where there are various activities, a physically and emotionally safe environment, support from adults, and plans for conflict resolution, students can learn, practice, or refine their social and emotional skills in a real-world setting. Adult presence can offer support and modeling of social and emotional skills during this time, without following a specific curriculum. However, even though social and emotional skills are necessary for students to engage positively at recess, throughout the school day, and in life, recess is often overlooked as an opportunity in the school day to build these skills.

SEL programs have measurable positive effects on students' emotional wellness, behavior, and academic performance.[12] First, they generate their intended results in terms of students' skills, attitudes, and positive social behaviors in social and emotional domains—such as emotion recognition, stress management, empathy, problem solving, and decision-making. They also reduce problem behaviors and misconduct as well as reduce emotional distress. SEL programs are also associated with gains in student academic performance. Importantly, these findings held for students of all ages and living in a variety of geographic locations.

> **At-a-Glance: Findings from the Playworks randomized controlled trial**
>
> Relative to control schools, Playworks schools experienced the following in one year:
> - Forty-three percent less bullying and discipline issues, as reported by teachers
> - Twenty percent greater student feelings of safety on the playground, as reported by teachers
> - Thirty-four percent less time spent transitioning back to class after recess
> - Forty-three percent more time spent in vigorous physical activity during recess

My own and others' research shows that with organized recess, students do learn social and emotional skills that align with what the literature identifies as important for long-term success. One such study is the randomized controlled trial of Playworks conducted by Mathematica Policy Research in collaboration with my team of researchers at the John W. Gardner Center for Youth and Their Communities at Stanford University. This study was critical for establishing the approach designed by the program as an evidence-based model for improving recess and school climate.[13] As a result of this study, Playworks was identified as a tier 1 social and emotional learning intervention for elementary schools.[14]

The study focused on schools in six regions and within districts, randomized some schools to the "treatment" condition (implementing the program during the school year) and some to the "control" condition (waiting one year to implement).[15] Findings demonstrated many positive effects of the program, including on students' social and emotional skill development, among other outcomes.[16] For example, we found a positive impact on teachers' reports of students' use of positive language and teachers' perceptions of whether students felt safe at school in general and at recess in particular. Teachers in treatment schools were also less likely to report bullying and exclusive behavior at recess than those in control schools. Transitions back to the classroom after recess took less time in these schools compared to control schools, and both teachers and students in treatment schools reported better behavior and attention in class after recess compared to those in control schools. Other research corroborates these findings. Using data from the statewide California Healthy Kids Survey, researchers found that students in Playworks schools reported increases over six years in their confidence in their social and emotional skills, whereas student reports in other schools declined during the period.[17]

The randomized controlled trial also used accelerometers as a way of tracking students' physical activity, and findings demonstrated the positive effects of the program for girls, in particular, who were more likely to be physically engaged through jump rope, tag, and other games than those in control schools.[18] It was also effective for African American and Latinx students, who gained more steps and time in moderate to vigorous physical activity in treatment schools.[19]

These findings are based on quantitative analyses of teacher and student surveys as well as data collected through tracking devices. These data sources can lack nuance or the ability to explain why such a finding might exist. In the rest of the chapter, I use examples from the many schools I've visited to help shed light on how reforming recess in the ways I've suggested can yield the kinds of social and emotional outcomes that educators are hoping to accrue. The findings suggest that even incremental improvements to recess can have lasting effects. Recess does not have to be perfect for students to learn and practice their social and emotional skills.

Social and Emotional Learning Embedded in Recess

At Thompson Elementary School, located in an urban metropolis, nearly all the students are African American, and most receive free and reduced-price meals. The principal, Mr. Butler, was in his second year at the school when my team and I visited. Thompson had implemented a version of Playworks called TeamUp that school year. They used their own staff—specifically teachers who taught special classes like art and physical education as well as administrators—as recess monitors trained by a Playworks coach who rotated between four schools, coming to Thompson one week out of every month. In the intervening weeks, Thompson recess staff worked on creating an organized, inclusive, positive, and safe recess yard for their students. In the year I visited Thompson Elementary, I also visited five other schools nationwide implementing the same program, including Culligan Elementary and Northside Elementary, where Coach Diana worked. Although the changes to recess took longer to stick without a full-time Playworks coach at the school every day, the research demonstrated the value of having the school "own" recess and take charge of making it a productive time for its students by embedding it in and aligning it with existing school values and programs.[20] Foundational parts of the programming involve supporting student engagement in play by incorporating positive messaging, inclusive behavior, a noncompetitive play yard, adult engagement, and simple conflict resolution to keep the game going. Each of these strategies helps to build students' social and emotional skills and offer scaffolded opportunities to practice SEL.

At Thompson School, Principal Butler described to me why he brought on the TeamUp program that year, focusing not only on what it would do for recess but also what it might do for the school as a whole when recess is better functioning:

> *I was hoping they could help us build a stronger school culture . . . and specifically working on stronger culture at recess. We have . . . this is a school community that, when I came into this school, had more fights than days of school and was largely described by parents, teachers, and everyone else as "the kids are running the school" literally and in terms of who was in charge here. We tried to do a lot last year to shift the culture. It felt like a five-year journey to get there, but I knew that one area that we were seeing a lot of challenges [was] at recess and lunch. I figured bringing in Playworks would help us address more organization, build a culture around it. I really like some of the models how peers handle conflicts.*

In reflecting further on how this approach has worked at his school, Principal Butler continued:

> *We started with a very strong training, and most of the staff were really, really energized about this new model of recess. When you*

> don't have a level organization of recess, it's even more stressful. ...
> Everyone was really welcoming for it. Then over the course of the
> year we had ups and downs. We had some holes in our system where
> what do we do when one person's absent. ... It's not like we just have
> a bench of people that we can just pull and plug in.

Principal Butler was very aware of the challenges his school faced, and he went on to name a few more but in the same interview also recounted the successes they had in terms of student engagement and student social and emotional learning. For instance, he counted as a success their implementation of the junior coach program. Junior coaching is an opportunity for upper-grade students to gain leadership skills by working at their own or younger students' recesses to lead games, set up and put away equipment, and interact with students of all ages. Principal Butler explained that he could not allow his junior coaches to be excused from class time to work at younger students' recesses because none of his students was meeting the grade-level state standards and they all needed the instructional time. Instead, at Thompson the junior coaches were responsible for equipment and play yard setup, a job they did during part of their lunchtime, which helped the teachers who would be supervising recess when it began. Principal Butler acknowledged that this was just one aspect of the program, but all they could manage in that year, and still he felt it was skill building for the students involved as the only leadership opportunity at the school:

> I do think even that role has been good for them. ... I feel like this
> opportunity has helped them grow a bit and mature a bit and take on
> responsibility, enjoy school more, all those sorts of things.

A kindergarten teacher at Thompson was excited about the new recess approach, understanding, as most early childhood educators do, that play is essential for learning at that age:

> Play, some people take that word for granted, like nothing's going
> on but fun. Through play, children are learning social skills, they're
> learning academics, and at five and six years old, I think more play
> needs to be brought into the program, but here we're moving away

> *from that. I roll with the way the school district says it should roll. We're trying to close an achievement gap. I understand that, but I believe play should be a bigger role in kindergarten.... Teaching the children how to play games where no one is a loser, everybody wins by playing, and following rules.*

She believed that TeamUp was good for her students. She was not part of the recess monitoring team, but she kept close track of what was happening at recess by connecting with her students as well as one of the teachers who was part of the monitoring team:

> *We want the structure to keep the kids safe, because without that guidance in play, they wrestle, which leads to serious fights and injuries. I know they're excited when we can get out and it's a good weather day where they can go out and play. I know when I pick them up; by the time they're finished, they're ... ready to go. For transitions, that's good for me.*

Based on my own observations, I would call the recess reform efforts at Thompson Elementary a moderate success. My team observed engagement in games and activities and adults interacting in positive ways with children, but also a fair amount of conflict and some examples of students being very unkind to one another. Key aspects of recess reform, including a schoolwide conflict resolution strategy, were not yet in place. I have no frame of reference for what the school looked like previously, but by all accounts, recess experienced vast improvements over what had been in place the prior year. Students confirmed what the adults reported; in a focus group with the junior coaches, we learned that they felt students were "acting nicer" to each other and that before "our school was very mean." They also were happy that they had more to do, more games set up, and lots of choices, whereas before there was nothing set up and so less opportunity to play and less opportunity to learn to resolve conflicts, interact with others, and take turns.

Culligan Elementary also implemented TeamUp in that same year and was part of the study. I characterize their program as more strongly implemented, including the junior coach program, because those students were allowed to work at younger students' recess periods. The assistant principal, Ms. Clark, was responsible for overseeing program implementation, including supervising the recess coach who had been hired that year to implement the program. Assistant Principal Clark described a way that she felt junior coaches had used a challenge during the year for a learning opportunity, not only for themselves, but also for other students:

> *The kids were coming out and they were super excited, but there was a lot of cheating kinds of behaviors going on.... Then the junior coaches... we had a couple of students come and present to me that they were feeling a little frustrated. Could they do an assembly, kind of a public service announcement so they needed to remind the kids about how to be safe and respectful and responsible? They generated the script... and then I helped them see that to reality.*

Through this leadership opportunity, students were able to identify a problem at their school, approach an administrator to express themselves, come up with a potential solution, and communicate with other students about the problem in an effort to resolve it. This experience afforded a tremendous opportunity for growth for these junior coaches, who without TeamUp would not have had any opportunities for leadership development at the school.

In other schools that implemented a fuller Playworks model that included an on-site coach who was trained to support a positive, safe, and engaged recess yard, the benefits to students' social and emotional learning were apparent. A principal at one of these schools that had very strongly implemented the program during the year reflected on the ways that it had integrated with another behavioral program at his school to support students' social and emotional learning:

> *We're using our system of PBIS here—you know, the Positive Behavioral Intervention [and Supports] plans. And if you're teaching kids proper behaviors, those are behaviors they eventually internalize. So, I think it... the program itself... complements what we're trying to do, in terms of the behaviors that we're trying to teach kids. Because one thing that I know is part of that program, we...*

> *Coach [name] teaches behaviors that can make kids successful while they're playing in the playground, and how to communicate with each other and how to act with each other.*

This principal went on to describe the downside, for his students, of changing their behaviors at school, because their existing behaviors might be more appropriate for survival outside of school:

> *Well, those are the same types of things that we're trying to do in the classroom, as far as behavior... positive behaviors are concerned. We don't try to eliminate behaviors that... because children bring behaviors to school that are good for them in the neighborhood and at home, and they work for them, so we don't want to eliminate those behaviors. Those behaviors may not be the most positive in school, but it works for them. So, here, our role is to change those by adding new behaviors to them. And the program, Playworks, by adding all of the things that they teach to kids, it just complements what we're doing here.*

This is a good example of why recess reform efforts need to be flexible and tailored to the needs of the student population at school. In this school, students were essentially being taught to "code switch," where they learned a set of behaviors and skills that would help them in the school environment but not untaught the skills and behaviors they might need for survival outside of school. These are strategies to support resilience for children who live in unsafe communities.

A teacher at this same school felt that the program was helpful to her students with the most needs for social and emotional skill building:

> *I have a few who, you know, I knew they didn't work that well with other people... who really, legitimately, right now, don't know how to play a cooperative game. And when they don't get their way, they don't "win," quote, unquote, even though none of these games have winners; if they think they are not winning, they will refuse to participate. And so, it's been kind of this experience of giving them a space to sort of try and work out some of those issues that they have with that.*

She also saw the inclusive and positive messaging that the program had tried to embed in recess carry over into her classroom:

> *I think some of the Playworks sort of philosophies and stuff sort of get embedded in the day, to sort of cooperate and get along and "high five" your buddy and support each other kind of thing, definitely.*

Importantly, we found that schools did not need to have their recess reforms solidly in place for some of these benefits to accrue. At Thompson and many other schools my team visited, the recess culture was still evolving. In some cases, recess monitors continued to be aloof, or conflict resolution had not been formally integrated. In many schools, inclusive and positive behavior—some of the hardest play yard behaviors to change—had not taken root. Yet even in these schools, administrators, teachers, and students overwhelmingly reported that recess felt better to them, there was more fun to be had, and student behavior was improved both at recess and in class.

Playworks set out to capture some of these effects and, in the program's annual staff survey, asked school employees (including administrators, counselors, teachers, monitors, and other staff) a series of questions about the extent to which they agreed with statements about how the program had affected their school, recess, and their students. In 2018, the majority of staff in schools that had implemented TeamUp, the lower-dosage model, felt that it had added to SEL. These data were not meant to measure the amount of change over the school year, but just the extent to which having the program made the school environment better or worse. This survey is not the gold standard of scientific research that the randomized controlled trial was, but it is evidence that educators feel that reforming recess is important in supporting specific aspects of SEL.

Conflict Resolution and Social and Emotional Learning at Recess

When students' social and emotional skills are underdeveloped, it is difficult for them to make good decisions about who and what to play with or

> **Findings from the 2017–18 Playworks school staff survey**
>
> Among the more than three thousand respondents in TeamUp schools:
> - Ninety-seven percent of school personnel felt the program resulted in more opportunities for inclusion at recess.
> - Ninety-two percent of school personnel reported that students were better able to resolve their own conflicts.
> - Eighty-six percent of school personnel reported fewer bullying incidents.
> - Eighty-five percent of school personnel reported fewer verbal and physical conflicts.
> - Ninety-three percent of teachers reported more cooperation.
> - Ninety-one percent of teachers reported better concentration for their students.
> - Eighty-one percent of teachers reported fewer class disruptions.

to manage their emotions if things do not go their way. The links between SEL and conflict at recess are very strong, and reduced conflict is one of the most commonly mentioned outcomes associated with recess reform, according to the many administrators and teachers with whom my team has spoken. Disagreement is part of play, and no recess reform can eliminate it; we would expect to see students disagree about issues such as whether a ball is in or out, who goes first in a game, or even what game to play. However, small disagreements can balloon into larger problems and end up derailing play, frustrating students, and creating emotional or physical safety issues. With attention to managing conflict using some fairly straightforward tools, these problems can be avoided or resolved, and students can learn to self-regulate and compromise so that they may continue playing.

The randomized controlled trial of Playworks demonstrated that the program results in a decrease in teacher reports of student bullying, a somewhat surprising finding given that the program is not an antibullying program, and none of its messages is specifically about bullying. A few teachers specifically mentioned bullying to us in interviews, but many talked about different kinds of conflicts that arose and how the tools that the program brought to bear were helping. For example, one teacher explained her view of the relationship between SEL and conflict:

> *Sometimes also when something will happen during recess where kids are calling ... a kid is calling another kid a name or there's some sort of fight that breaks out, that it impacts kind of like the whole class's emotions and socially, coming back into the classroom.*

At another school, a teacher described how she worked with the recess coach at her school to help her students deescalate the emotional and sometimes physical conflict that she observed with her students in class and also headed out to the recess yard:

> *Before, name calling, a lot of tattling was happening. I actually had them getting physical with each other, not in the classroom but as soon as they would go outside the door, they would be, like, pushing each other. And it was just getting really vicious. Like I said, they were calling each other "rivals" and "enemies." And they were saying, "I hate you!" And it was just pretty nasty. . . . Well, I have been working since the beginning of the year to teach them about respecting each other. And then when Coach [name] came in, I asked him to help me with that. So, both of us talking, a lot of the rivals are no longer rivals; now, they're best friends. And, I mean, there's a lot less meanness, I could say. There's a lot less calling each other bad words. And they have matured a bit because of it.*

This example illustrates the ways that the more structured classroom behavioral expectations can limit students' abilities to practice their social and emotional skills. By coordinating with the recess coach, this teacher was able to scaffold her SEL efforts in class with opportunities for practice at recess, and she found that to be successful with her students.

She was not the only teacher to mention transitions as a time when students needed help in making good decisions. Another teacher described a similar problem with students so excited to go to recess that they physically pushed each other to get out the door and then back in again:

> So, at the beginning of the year, like I said, they would . . . push each other about being first in line and being first in the classroom. Now, they're more harmonious. . . . I think all of this talk about respect and getting along with each other is finally starting to get in their heads. Like, "You can't be treating each other like this!"

By having aligned strategies for classroom and recess behaviors, especially positive behavior messages about being respectful and treating each other kindly, this teacher felt that her students were able to turn around their behavior and at the same time improve her own experiences with recess transitions. Without the physical pushing, she had a much easier time transitioning her students from class to the yard and back again.

At Thompson Elementary, Principal Butler noted that one of the challenges they faced in implementing recess reforms was conflict resolution. TeamUp recommends a simple-to-use strategy of rock-paper-scissors (also known as ro-sham-bo) to resolve basic conflicts that arise in any game, such as who goes first and whether the ball is in or out. Principal Butler says they did not even get that far in their first year of implementation:

> If there's a component of the program that I would like to see moving forward that we do, that we really prioritize the focus on, it's on that. I don't even think we got to training students or supporting students with ro-sham-bo as a conflict strategy. We didn't even get to that.

Still, he felt that recess was vastly improved in terms of conflict. He went on to say, "We've had far, far, far less fights happen at recess than not," comparing his recess experience this year to the prior year. A few students were still regularly having trouble during recess time, however. Principal Butler described how they handled those few children at every recess who simply could not abide by the rules and interact positively with other students because their social and emotional skills were so underdeveloped:

> When you are a student that has multiple triggers, and then you're maybe outside with sixty, seventy students, that's a bit much. We pull and we have an alternative recess where there are between nine and twelve students. They're still playing. They're still playing some of the same exact

games, but they're just in a smaller space and it's just a smaller number of them. That happens at the tennis court area or in the gym.

We did not hear about this particular approach to SEL at any other school, but Principal Butler had an especially acute sense of what SEL means. During one of the days we visited, he was shadowed by a young boy all day, wherever he went, including monitoring recess (the principal was responsible for overseeing basketball). When I asked him later why this boy was out at all the recess periods, he told me that the boy had been suspended for attacking another child and could not go back to class. But his parent wasn't able to pick him up until after her work shift ended. Rather than keep the child locked in a detention room alone all day, Principal Butler had the boy shadow him and allowed the boy to play basketball (closely monitored) at the recesses, demonstrating to him what social and emotional skills look like in the hopes that the boy could take this back with him to class when his suspension was over.

Many other principals in the schools I visited also embraced SEL at recess. A principal at another school recounted what happened before his attempts at recess reform:

The biggest thing is that they would, for example, if they were playing basketball, like the fourth- and fifth-grade boys, they would play basketball and they would change the rules during the game or play by different rules. And then, they would get into full-on fights over what the outcome of the game should be or shouldn't be, if the ball was in or out. They would have a fistfight over it. So, they really just didn't understand how do you navigate when you don't agree on something? How do you navigate coming up with the rules of a game on the yard? And those were just some of the basics with our fourth and fifth graders.... The two years before I came, they had the highest suspension rate in our school district.

This principal went on to describe how changing the culture of recess through the kinds of reform efforts I have documented reverberated for his students—improving inclusion and engagement as well as reducing conflict.

These sentiments are borne out in the survey of school staff administered by Playworks each year. Again, focusing on schools with TeamUp, a lower-dosage model of the program, staff in 2017–18 reported a strong influence of the program on their students' behavioral outcomes. Eighty-six percent of staff reported fewer bullying incidents, and 85 percent reported fewer verbal and physical conflicts. These staff perceptions are difficult to bear out with data collected on disciplinary incidents in schools because those incidents are not universally recorded or recorded in the same way. Some schools have data systems that track every referral to the office, and many do not. Schools have different cultures toward referrals also, with some resolving conflicts on the spot where they occur and others sending any kind of conflict to the office for resolution. More and more, schools are turning to restorative practices that sometimes include a reflection room where students can work through problems with a counselor, and again these instances may or may not be tracked as disciplinary issues. In short, the teacher perceptions reported in the survey are probably the best evidence we have that reforming recess, even incrementally, can improve disciplinary problems.

Adults and Student Social and Emotional Learning at Recess

Adult presence, actions, and interactions at recess can strongly support or detract from students' social and emotional learning. In the worst-case scenario, adults exert their authority through yelling at or berating students rather than modeling for them what healthy interactions look like. The next worst scenario is when they simply ignore students. We saw examples of both of these adult issues, and principals also noted them—for example, as described by a principal at one school:

> *We had some accountability issues with folks, I don't know, sort of engaging with the students like take a seat. Just got finished teaching two hours' worth of class where you were doing something stressful and now you're outside, a little bit of fresh air, you're not really engaged with the students or you're checking a text message, or whatever the case may be.*

These are missed opportunities for supporting students' SEL at recess. Adults have the opportunity to engage with students in ways that model positive communication, build rapport and relationships, demonstrate inclusive behavior, and assist when needed to resolve conflicts. When adults engage with students in these ways at recess, everyone benefits. As one principal told us, in reference to his team of two recess coaches employed by the school:

> *What's nice about it is that—is they interact with the kids enough to know their names and they're also our crossing guards, so they see them in that respect also. So they kind of have a relationship in both ways with them.*

When these relationships are solidified, the recess coach can become one of the most revered staff members at school, earning so-called rock star status, as we heard in many schools. The recess staff may be the only staff who see every child every day, and this affords them a strong basis for building relationships with students. At some of the schools we visited, Playworks ran afterschool sports leagues for students. This additional time with students was seen as improving their relationships and also adding to student success by encouraging students to come to school. One teacher told us:

> *Another aspect of it are these special afterschool programs that they run: the basketball, the volleyball. And the kids absolutely love that, and it's just a great special thing to offer to the kids and the families, and it's the kind of thing that helps students' attendance, it helps their attitude toward school, it helps their social skills and their health.*

In fact, in a study that examined attendance at Playworks and non-Playworks schools in two districts, implementing the program was associated with a small but statistically significant increase in student attendance.[21] Several hypotheses could explain this result, including that students want to come to school because they feel connected to an adult at recess, that they feel safer at recess, or that they look forward to their specific games. In all cases, what adults are doing matters.

Administrators' Roles in Creating Supportive Recess

Adult roles go beyond those at recess, however. Administrators play a huge role in creating recess environments that are supportive to children at school. At a school that had recently brought back recess after several years without a recess in the bell schedule, the principal talked about her role in supporting the implementation of a supportive recess:

> *Well, the first year I came here, there was a lot of emphasis on culture and climate, building those healthy, positive attitudes about learning. And there were a lot of procedures, policies, practices that needed to be developed and established. So, there had to be a lot to do with organization. And, yes, there have been a lot of changes since I've been here.... The instruction, the curriculum planning, yes, that's all important, but I think we missed an opportunity at the beginning of the year to spend more time getting to know our students and letting them get to know us.*

Another principal also recognized her role in recess reform, taking responsibility for "creating" a playground environment, rather than letting it create itself:

> *I think it was just this whole idea of how do we really create a playground that is fully inclusive of all of our students. Really wanting to create a climate and structured situations out there where all kids could have a place to go to if they chose to or needed extra support getting engaged and active on the playground. That's what our motivation [was].*

These principals saw their own role in recess reform as essential for setting the tone and creating a recess period that meets students' SEL needs. Not all principals had that same vision for their own role. Instead, they relied on others to implement recess reform and, as observers rather than supporters, were less familiar with what was happening. Recess reform can take root in these cases too, but where principals are actively engaged, they are aware of the changes happening and can use their authority to align that work with other SEL or school climate initiatives happening at school.

Overall School Climate and Social and Emotional Learning at Recess

Social and emotional learning is an individual-level concept. Although social skills require interaction with others, social and emotional learning refers to development of the student as an individual and not a collective set of skills that a class or a grade or a school acquires. These more school-level concepts are also important, however, because "school climate" is also a key predictor of student success and is strongly linked to SEL at school.[22] School climate refers to environmental factors such as policies, practices, and norms that support, collectively, students' feelings of emotional and physical safety; student engagement and mutual respect; collaborations among students, families, and educators; and student and school staff contribution to school functioning.[23] Although as concepts SEL and school climate may require different approaches, they share a set of outcomes, including supportive adult-student and peer-to-peer relationships, physical and emotional safety, and student engagement.[24] A school that successfully integrates SEL with school climate will have schoolwide values that are articulated to and embraced by students and staff—such as respect, responsibility, fairness, honesty—and convey to students an overall purpose for attending school.[25]

In the first study of Playworks I conducted, my team and I observed an entire year of recess reform efforts at six low-income elementary schools in the Silicon Valley region. At the end of that year, we reflected on the data collections and identified a set of criteria that established a "high-quality" recess: (1) appropriate games, space, and equipment were made available to students; and (2) adults intentionally supported students' development of pro-social skills.[26] We felt that four of the six schools we followed in that year had reached a high-quality recess, and the other two were still in process for a few reasons, including underlying administrative problems at the school that were unrelated to recess reform efforts, coach turnover during the year, and lack of staff buy-in for the changes. At the end of the year we surveyed teachers at all six schools asking about, among other items, their perceptions of the overall school climate. We found strong statistical evidence, backed by findings from the interviews and focus groups, that having

> **Social-emotional learning and positive school climate share these outcomes**
>
> - supportive relationships
> - engagement
> - physical and emotional safety
> - cultural competence and responsiveness
> - challenge and high expectations

a strong recess culture was associated with a stronger school climate. This point is important because the school climate literature tends to overlook recess as a place where children can feel emotionally and physically safe (or not), engage with others (or not), and feel part of a shared vision for behavioral expectations and norms around play (or not). Recess climate is interwoven with school climate in such a way that it would be impossible to have a positive school climate in the presence of a negative recess climate.

Playworks leadership has understood this for some time. A regional executive director who oversaw program operations through his region expressed the sentiment this way:

> *The other issue is, and we talk about this among Playworks is, if a school really values improving school climate and they see play as being a vital component in shifting school culture, you can't really have the mind frame that you're always going to just contract that out. It trickles down throughout the school community, and you get less investment from teachers and paraprofessionals to really support what it is that we're trying to do, is transforming school climate through creating a positive recess.*

He's describing why Playworks cannot always just put the program's own staff into a school and expect school climate to change. Instead, he's making an argument for having school staff and leadership take ownership of the recess reform process and align it with other schoolwide programs so that everyone, from the administration to the teachers to the paraprofessionals, supports the process. If it's contracted out, as he says, it can be harder to get that buy-in for making schoolwide changes.

One principal noticed a big change at recess climate when her school implemented TeamUp. The school, located in the outskirts of a major city in the West, had about half its students from the surrounding neighborhood and the other half coming from around the school district to be part of a magnet gifted and talented program. In the past, the principal told us, the neighborhood students would play at recess, but the magnet program children would not:

> When I first came, I noticed there was like a division. The neighborhood kids, lots of physical activity, and I actually would walk outside and there would be a lot of kids just sitting and visiting and books outside. Once I got to know the school, it was largely our [gifted and talented] ... kids. We noticed when Playworks came in, it leveled the playing field a little bit because there were ... options other than soccer, football, basketball, which maybe they haven't had a lot of experience with. That's not their area. Just as far as knowing the rules for four-square or some of the other Playworks games, the tag games seem to get them more involved. I saw it increase from what it was, because it was pretty obvious last year, or the first year I was here.

This school participated in TeamUp, where Playworks supported one of the school's own recess monitors to take over the recess program to introduce new games with common rules, create an inclusive and positive play yard, focus on conflict resolution, and interact with students through play. Coach Helen, a former stay-at-home mom with middle-school-aged children, started the position in the beginning of the school year. Her own children were at a school with Playworks, and she learned about the program from them before she even started her job. According to the program staff member who supported Coach Helen, she was doing a great job at the school. Coach Helen noticed changes in the student activity spurred by her efforts:

> Kids used to read books. They [would] hang out at the wall and complain there was nothing to do. They kind of forgot how to play ... that when they come out, they're supposed to play. They're supposed to run. They're supposed to jump. They're supposed to do things. And also there's less discipline problems because of the fact that they have something to do, and we don't see folks coming out or kids just sitting on a stair. You know, is it time to go in yet? They are learning to play.

The junior coach program was robust, and fourth- and fifth-grade students were allowed to work at their own and younger students' recess periods. The focus group with these students yielded consistent messages about their jobs. One student said:

> We try and do everything in our ability to help kids, to make kids have fun, to bring them, like, closer together as friends. We try and do everything we can to include all of them.

Another added, "We try to stop bullying," and a third interjected:

> So it's not—we're not really antibullying. We're more like trying to help people so that they're, like, friends or, like, that they can play together in a nice way.

These junior coaches especially liked their role with younger students and talked about their interactions with great pride:

> It's also awesome to work with other kids that you [wouldn't] really, like, usually know because you're in that grade and they're in a different grade and, like, you can become friends with more people since you're playing with them.

When asked how recess reform and Coach Helen had changed their school, one student responded:

> Playworks has changed our school so much by helping kids, like, do fun ... more fun activities, even inside recess. ... Playworks' job is to make kids love what they want to do most right now and that is play.

These examples point to the ways that reforming recess can not only improve students' individual social and emotional competencies but also help the school overall to become a more welcoming, safe, and comfortable place for students and staff. Efforts to create a positive school climate are present in many schools through formal programs like character education to informal approaches like school mottos and pride. It is impossible to have a positive school climate if students feel excluded, threatened, or unwelcome at recess. A strong recess climate is an integral part of a strong school climate. Aligning school climate-promoting efforts with recess reform will solidify recess as a place that school climate is formed and will help school staff understand that even if they are not present at recess, what happens there affects their students throughout the school day.

PART III

Supporting Recess Through Policy and Practice

CHAPTER SIX

Local Policies and Practices to Support Recess

Imagine the midday scene at most elementary schools. Students have been inside their classrooms since early in the morning and are eager to get on their feet and move around. Some are hungry, especially if they did not have the opportunity to eat breakfast at home and were not offered a morning meal or snack at school. Others want to get right down to the business of meeting their friends and playing their favorite games outside. Schools usually block time for lunch and recess back to back, but how to structure this time and how to incorporate the needs of multiple classes and grade levels are important questions. For instance, which should come first—the eating or the playing—and how much time should be allotted to each? Should each grade level have its own recess, or should they be combined or overlapped somehow? These scheduling decisions can seem mundane, but they do have an effect on both recess and lunch functioning and, by extension, student health and well-being.

Decisions about policy and practice that govern recess time for children are made at the local level, either school by school or district by district. Policy, in this case, is not necessarily legislation or official regulations, but rather what the school leaders decide is "how they do things" at the school. Decisions made by local leadership at the school or the district level are essential for creating the conditions and supports needed for a productive recess, and most of these can be revised, removed, or enforced by local leadership. It may be that informal tradition rather than intention guide school practices, that schools are scheduling lunch and recess in the ways that they do not because they have weighed alternatives, but because that's how it has always been. In this chapter, I explore how to optimize the policies and practices that govern recess to ensure a better experience for all students. I focus on two key areas where local decision-making matters: scheduling and staffing. These may not be the most exciting aspects of recess reform to consider, but they are the behind-the-scenes supports necessary to ensure an engaged and productive recess for students.

Recess Scheduling

Creating the bell schedule in a school is an unenviable task. Meeting requirements for instructional blocks and moving large groups of children from place to place safely and with appropriate supervision are challenging. Yet, these are vitally important tasks for the school principal, and how the schedule plays out has major impacts on student learning. Although recess may not be at the top of the list of priorities when scheduling decisions are made, in this section I lay out three scheduling issues that should be considered by local decision makers in planning for an organized and productive recess: the timing of eating and playing at lunch recess, the amount of recess time that should be built into the bell schedule, and considerations for combining grade levels at recess time.

Eat or Play First at Midday Break?

Nearly every elementary school schedules recess and lunch together at midday. Sometimes other recess periods are also scheduled during the school day, but in schools that have regularly scheduled recess, lunchtime is the most common time of day for it to occur. Traditionally, students eat first and then spend the rest of their time playing, but in the past decade, school health practitioners have begun to promote play first to help students eat more food at lunch and feel better and more energized while playing at recess. Foremost have been concerns about children's midday eating habits and food waste, spurred the hypothesis that when lunch comes before recess, some students will rush through their meal and even skip eating so that they can get to the play yard more quickly. This scenario is especially problematic because evidence strongly confirms that adequate nutrition is essential for children's cognitive development;[1] furthermore, being hungry is associated with difficulty in paying attention and behavioral disruptions in class.[2] Rushing through lunch might help students get out to recess faster, but it may also derail their learning, and possibly that of others, later in the day when hungry children have trouble concentrating and behaving.

Research demonstrates the validity of the hypothesis that having recess first and lunch second leads to less food waste and more food consumption overall. Across a series of small-scale studies emerges a set of fairly consistent findings demonstrating that when students play first and then eat, they tend to eat more calories, drink more milk, and waste less of their school lunch.[3]

Some schools require students to sit at lunch for a mandated block of time (e.g., fifteen minutes) before they are released to play to ensure they have adequate time for everyone to finish eating. This mandate may not solve the problem, however, because some of the most active children know or experience that running on a full stomach will make them feel sick.[4] If their primary goal is to run and be active at recess, eating just beforehand might limit this goal. Indeed, the research demonstrates a stronger effect of playing before eating among older elementary boys, who tend to be the most active during recess.[5] They eat less when lunch comes before recess than when it is offered in the reverse.

There is some evidence that whether children should eat or play first depends on how long they have to do each. With a longer combined recess and lunch period, students are more physically active when they eat before playing.[6] However, in shorter combined recess and lunch periods, children are more active when they play before eating. The reason may be that children are hungry when they come out and playing first prolongs that hunger even more in a longer recess.

The shift from "eat then play" to "play then eat" is starting to take hold in elementary schools; according to the 2016 School Health Policies and Practices survey, 8 percent of school districts now require that schools schedule recess prior to lunch, and an additional 22 percent of districts recommend that practice.[7]

Still, there are documented challenges for making this approach work. Foremost among these is whether having students play before they eat will disadvantage lower-income or food insecure students who have not eaten breakfast at home before school and rely on their school lunch for their main meal. For these students, waiting an extra fifteen or twenty minutes to eat could be physically unhealthy, and being hungry will likely diminish their ability to enjoy recess and practice skills like self-regulation. If schools offer free breakfast or a midmorning snack, delaying lunch until after recess may not be a problem. My advice is to tailor school policy and practice to the school environment, taking into account food access and security among the student population in making scheduling decisions about when to eat and play.

A second concern is how to make sure students are hygienic when they sit down to eat after playing at recess. Are there handwashing stations, time for all students to use the restroom, or other mechanisms that can be put in place to ensure hygiene standards are met at lunchtime? Other logistical concerns include what students should do with their outerwear at lunch: do they hang up their jackets and then go into lunch, and if so, who monitors them while they are doing that? What about students who need to stop and pick up their sack lunches? Barriers noted by research focus heavily on supervisory issues, such as whether enough staff are available to both walk students inside to lunch and watch students coming out to recess at the same time.[8]

One area that research has not considered in detail, but that I think is a potential problem, is that when students have recess-time problems that they need help to resolve, they often turn to their teacher. If students go straight to lunch, who will help them to resolve their lingering conflicts—if they exist—so that they can settle down to eat? Perhaps with organized recess, these conflicts will be minimized and this problem will resolve itself, but all these issues must be attended to if eating before playing is implemented. Convening a task force that includes key stakeholders such as administration, teachers, recess and lunch monitors, and students is one way to ensure that these challenges are addressed appropriately for the school culture and student population.

While the research has focused on the timing of lunch and recess and food consumption, it has not considered whether eating or playing first makes a difference in recess-related outcomes, such as student enjoyment and social and emotional learning. Although the recess-before-lunch schedule makes a lot of sense from a nutrition and food waste perspective, and possibly also from a physical activity perspective, from a recess functioning and social-emotional development perspective, we do not have much information about whether these scheduling decisions impact students' recess experiences.

How Much Recess Is the Right Amount?

A 2014 article in the *Atlantic* documented one American teacher's challenge when first teaching in an elementary school in Finland.[9] Finnish teachers gave their elementary students a fifteen-minute break for each forty-five- to sixty-minute block of instruction, and this American teacher could not imagine how the business of teaching and learning could be completed with so much recess taking place. Perhaps it won't surprise you that this teacher learned that providing many short breaks for students actually helped them to focus and learn better.

Finland, unlike the United States, embraces the notion that children need breaks in order to concentrate and learn. Although no national laws in Finland regulate how much and how often students need breaks, in practice, students in primary schools tend to have two to four recess periods of up to fifteen minutes per day in addition to a longer thirty-minute break around lunchtime.[10] Estimates from the 2010 Gallup/Robert Wood Johnson Foundation survey indicate that American students, especially those in low-income and urban schools, are not receiving anywhere near that much recess time. Finnish students might have two or more hours of breaks during the school day, and US students might have thirty minutes total, if they are lucky.

What is the optimal amount of recess, and how many recess periods should there be per day? Texas Christian University professor Deborah

> **Estimates of daily recess minutes from the Gallup/RWJF principal survey (2010)**
>
> - Fifty-six percent of schools provide thirty or fewer minutes.
> - Twenty-four percent of schools provide thirty to forty-five minutes.
> - Twenty percent of schools provide more than forty-five minutes.
> - In urban schools serving predominantly low-income students, 70 percent provide thirty or fewer minutes.

Rhea recommends four fifteen-minute breaks during the day, two before lunch and two after.[11] In the program she designed, the LiiNK Project, children experience these short recess bursts throughout the day, much like in Finland. Paired with a character development program, the LiiNK Project is showing promising results, such as improved social and emotional learning and academic outcomes, along with fewer classroom disruptions and more physical activity. Unlike Rhea's project, the report authored by the CDC and SHAPE America has a more modest recommendation—that all children should have recess every day for at least fifteen minutes, but then further suggests more than one fifteen-minute recess would be more developmentally appropriate.[12]

One fifteen-minute break in a six- to seven-hour school day seems like the absolute minimum that children need, although in most schools I visited, that was exactly what they had. However, every California school we visited had two recesses—one in the morning and one at lunch. Combined, these two periods equated to about thirty-five to forty minutes of recess per day. Regardless of geographic location, some teachers reported that they would take their children out for a break at other times as needed, but only for a special treat or if they felt like being outside.

Having scheduled breaks so that all children have the opportunity to play is a better policy for ensuring equity in access to recess than allowing teachers the option of a second or third recess when they feel they can manage it. A Playworks regional staff member interviewed in one of my studies spoke about the scheduling challenge and recess time like this:

> *The scheduling is a huge issue, and in a district here they have to have ninety minutes of literacy training and ninety minutes of math training a day. Most schools do that in the morning block. I mean, that is pushing a lot into small brains. So it's no wonder that by the time kids get out to recess, they're losing their beans, you know, and they're misbehaving or whatever because they're so pent up. So one of the things that I'm pushing is thirty minutes of recess a day because in most of our schools it's fifteen or maybe twenty, and you don't have to do it all at one block.*

Ultimately, it is the decision of the school principal how many breaks students receive and for how many minutes. The recommendation of the professionals is that having more breaks during the day is developmentally appropriate for young children and can help their attention and classroom behavior. The evidence suggests that there will not be any detrimental effects on academic learning from incorporating more breaks into the school day. In fact, it is likely that some teachers are already building these breaks into their daily schedules, whether they take their students outside to the yard to play or let them have a few minutes in class for a break. Good recess policy includes both the length and frequency of breaks for all students, ensuring equitable access to adequate breaks across classrooms.

Recess: Separate or Together?

Building school schedules is complicated, so how to schedule recess so that students get the most out of their time is likely not at the top of the priority list when schedules are being made. Blocks of time are needed for reading and math, as well as time for social studies and science, along with specials like art, music, and physical education. How to move children throughout the time available and ensure everyone has adequate stretches for academic and other kinds of learning is essential.

When it comes to scheduling recess, a number of decisions must be made. Several have been addressed in this chapter already: how many and how long should recess periods be, and should recess be scheduled before or after lunch? Other considerations include how many classes should be together at recess, whether they should all come out and leave at the same time or have staggered or overlapping breaks, and if grade levels are to be combined, which ones make sense to link together.

The space available for play is the key driver for how many students can be released at recess at once. If the school has a small outdoor play space or, if in a colder weather climate, inadequate indoor space, it may be that only one grade level can be released at a time. This means that some grades eat and play very early and others eat and play very late in the day, so if at all possible, scheduling multiple grade levels together is best. Most recesses I have observed that include multiple grade levels group consecutive grades together—first and second, third and fourth, and so on. This makes intuitive sense because children who are one grade level apart are likely to have similar interests and skill levels in terms of games and play. There are developmental reasons to think they will be good playmates and able to integrate across grade levels, more so than students of different age groups. But, context is important because, as we learned from Playworks regional staff in one city, this is not always the case:

> *One of my schools [has] fifth and sixth graders [together]. The girls are beating the crap out of each other. . . . They should have their own recess.*

Administrators told us that decisions to combine nonconsecutive grades at recess were made because of issues like this, where the students in two consecutive grades did not get along. They felt that if they separated the two grades into different recesses, disciplinary referrals from recess would be reduced.

At another school, we observed recesses that included students with nonconsecutive grade levels grouped together at recess, and this approach also had challenges. One recess combined kindergarteners with second-grade students for a fifteen-minute recess. Although these students are just two years apart, those two years are critical at this age in terms of developmentally appropriate games and expectations. The field notes from that recess read:

> *Two K kids come to [coach] right away and say that the older kids won't let them play soccer. She goes over to help them sort it out and reminds the second graders that they need to include the K kids,*

> which they do. But they still have a hard time because the littler kids cannot play soccer the way the older kids can, so [coach] helps them to come up with a game with the soccer ball that everyone can play.

This same recess observation goes on to describe separate play for the kindergarten and second-grade students in terms of the games students are interested in and the level at which they can play them. Tetherball is another example of a game that is not well integrated, and an imaginative game initiated by kindergarteners is similarly not well integrated. It may be fine to have two separate sets of recess activities, except with limited space and equipment this may unnecessarily restrict the kinds of play that can happen.

An advantage of the multiage recess is that it's an opportunity for older students to become mentors to younger ones, and both older and younger students gain in those relationships. In addition, younger and older siblings can be out at the same recess period, which again can lead to gains for both students. The main disadvantage is that students from different age groups have different interests and skill levels, and planning for a recess that suits two diverse sets of needs is difficult. Older students might want to play a serious basketball game that would be unsafe for younger children, and younger children might be most interested in tag games or jumping rope that would not be the choice for older students. Even if they play the same games, they would likely not play them in the same ways, limiting multiage interactions. If the space is large enough and the school has sufficient monitors or recess leaders to support two sets of recess games for different age groups, this arrangement can work. However, it makes the recess planning process considerably more complicated for school staff.

Overlapping Recess Periods Work for Scheduling but Not for Organized Recess

One strategy to reduce the span of time during which recess and lunch occur is to have overlapping recess periods where consecutive age groups come out to play in interspersed intervals. If first graders come out first, they may be at recess for ten minutes and then the second graders come out. Ten minutes later the first graders leave and the third graders arrive. In another ten minutes, the second graders leave and so on. This approach has the advantage of creating a shorter block of time during which all recess periods occur so that students are not eating overly early or late, which might be very important for large schools. For instance, field notes from one school's lunch recess observation read:

> *At this school the bell schedule is complicated, and lunch/recess for each grade level overlaps with others. Every five minutes another bell rings, followed by a whistle by a yard duty announcing which grade needs to line up and go in.*

Although I have never observed this rotation schedule from inside the cafeteria, I understand how it would align well with school lunch disbursement.

This strategy is, however, among the worst scheduling options for a productive recess time for children. The constant influx and outflow of students makes it difficult to sustain games. Students may have just gotten a large enough group for a tag game when half leave. The older students coming out may not be interested in the games of their younger peers and instead gravitate toward another activity. The constant movement of students in and out of the space also creates chaos as students run through each other's games to enter or leave. As researchers, we were woefully confused by the overlapping recess bell schedule, but sometimes students also weren't sure if their grade was supposed to leave when the bell rang, and monitors too were confused at times. In a visit to one school with an overlapping recess, for example, field notes read:

> *Another boy comes up to me and asks, "Was that the second- or third-grade bell?" Again, I have my schedule, so I tell him it was the second-grade bell; he keeps playing. [This bell schedule is REALLY confusing if you're not paying attention and counting each bell.]*

We did not ask respondents specifically about these kinds of schedules, but where schools had staggered schedules, it was clear that we, as observers, were not the only ones having problems keeping track of who was coming and going.

Having such rapid turnover also makes it difficult for games to be tailored specifically to certain age groups, including making sure that appropriate equipment is available for the games played by older or younger students. Monitors might want to put away hula hoops that younger children like when the older students come out so that those aren't misused by the older students and broken. They might want to put out cones for soccer or flags for flag football that aren't appropriate for younger age groups but, with the quick turnaround, may not have time to do this.

Most importantly, having staggered recesses creates challenges with transitions to and from recess. When half the recess yard leaves and half stays, the exiting students might not realize it's time to go or may resist leaving because they want to finish their game. It is more difficult for monitors to round up all the exiting students when stragglers won't come back inside with their classes. Staggered recesses work against the collective transition out of recess that I suggested aids an organized recess, where all students take a knee when time is up and then walk off the yard together. This cannot happen when only half the students are leaving recess at a time.

In short, a number of downsides to scheduling staggered recesses make it incompatible with the goals of an organized recess that supports students' social and emotional development. If at all possible, I recommend avoiding this way of scheduling students' recess periods.

Recess Staffing

Throughout the book I have mentioned the importance of administrative buy-in for recess changes as well as having someone on the ground at recess to implement the pieces of an organized recess. This administrator who has bought in to the importance of a well-run and productive recess could be called the "recess champion" or "manager," and the day-to-day person could be called the "recess coach." What does it take to have both these positions filled at every school?

My research teams learned a lot about the roles of recess champion and recess coach from talking to administrators within the Playworks program, who have worked for years with school personnel to bring recess reform to their schools. In this section, we rely on some of their insights to help make the case for the importance of both of these kinds of roles. The interviews took place in the context of a study of the program's TeamUp; my team set out to learn from these professionals about what they felt contributed to sustainable recess reforms at the school and district levels. The study focused on schools that used their own recess teams to implement an organized recess with strong support and coaching from a Playworks staff person, who visited each school for one week per month throughout the school year. The supervisor of that staff person and other regional staff were observers for this process who commented on what worked in making long-term change among the many schools they served.

The Important Role of a Recess Champion

The recess champion at a school can be any person who is in a leadership position or who is invested strongly in improving recess. In most schools my teams have visited, that person is the principal or assistant principal. In many cases, they had come from schools that had been working on recess and brought with them the learning experienced through those efforts. For instance, one principal heard about the program when he was a teacher earlier in his career and followed the progress of Playworks in his region before bringing it to his first job as a principal. In another school in an urban district, the recess champion was actually the school nurse. At Richard Babbitt Elementary School, Nurse Frank brought Playworks to the attention of the principal, Principal Russo, who agreed it was a good idea. Nurse Frank had apparently been focused on different ways to organize recess and learned about Playworks through his research. Having been at Richard Babbitt for twenty-five years, Nurse Frank was one of its most long-standing employees and someone who knew the school inside and out. Although Nurse Frank was not necessarily the decision maker at the school, he did write a small grant proposal to fund the work and acted as the key resource for the Playworks coach coming in. That coach explained:

> *Nurse Frank has been my, probably the most . . . the biggest resource at Richard Babbitt, to be honest. And he's helped me with everything, 'cause he's been pushing . . . he said he's been pushing a [more organized] recess for five years now, but it's been working on and off. So, that's what brought him to Playworks. But if there's ever any, you know, I need equipment, he always had, like, grant money*

or whatever to buy equipment. If there's issues with teachers or anything, he'll tell me the best way to go around it, 'cause he [has known] most of the staff for a really long time. So, he is definitely my biggest resource at Richard Babbitt.

A school nurse is an unusual recess champion, but not the only example of a nonadministrator in the recess champion role. In another school we visited, the behavior intervention specialist was the recess champion. She oversaw the school's two recess aides—both of whom were school district employees—and coordinated the parent volunteers who rotated through recess supervision duty. She herself was also out during recess providing support specifically for behavioral issues although she delegated the actual recess oversight to her team of employees and volunteers. Importantly, she was the key staff member to convince her principal to allow junior coaches to be present at both their own and younger students' recesses. These fifth-grade students had to miss some class time to do this, but she negotiated with the fifth-grade teaching team to allow these students to make up their classwork when they were at junior coach duty. On the days that we visited this school, we observed that junior coaches were indeed instrumental in helping to run an organized and engaged recess.

School District Partnerships for Continuity and Support

Staffing changes and administrator turnover at schools are notorious problems for all educational reforms, including recess reform. One leader's pet project passed down to a less enthusiastic leader can fall to the wayside in favor of the new leader's priorities. The executive director of one regional office we visited commented on the challenges faced when the school leader identified to spearhead the effort in the spring leaves by the time the recess reform effort is slated to begin the next fall:

Then, again, it sounds attractive in the spring when we're sitting at a table and we're having conversations about next year. When next year actually shows up . . . and she's like, oh, we're down an assistant principal, or oh, the person I thought was going to be the contact didn't come back this year. When the real life happens, what you

> talked about around the table in the spring is not what happens in truth in the fall. Then it's like there isn't the buy-in that we thought there was for the program.

One way to overcome this scenario is to embed recess reform at the district, rather than the school, level. Some schools we visited for this project had supportive districts that were willing to help fund the project or create systems so that recess reform could take place. In one district, for instance, a new climate and safety department in the district administrative office was seen as key for linking recess reform to district priorities. In another district, an initiative was in place to align physical education with recess curricula in an effort to improve both periods, capitalizing on what pilot schools were learning through their partnerships with Playworks to embed into districtwide curricula. In a third district, key leaders came from the recess reform movement and were the drivers of change, intentionally trying to saturate the district with improved recess for all elementary schools and students.

An advantage of partnering with the school district is the potential for aligning recess reforms with other reforms already underway. For example, one school district hired paraprofessionals for its schools to support cocurricular activities like arts, physical education, engineering, technology, and media library classes, which were then built into the school day. The district had not made the connection to recess, but a Playworks leader worked with district and school leadership to identify ways to promote recess organization and engagement through these district-sponsored cocurricular activities. They even found a way to capitalize on the staff that had been hired to support the district initiative. In another locale, we learned that alignment with PE reform was also key to supporting recess reform. A program director at a regional Playworks office told us:

> Part of that is the connection between PE and recess. That's a really easy one for schools to do because they're all doing PE anyway. If they explicitly message that these are skills that you're picking up, that you can take back out to recess, awesome. That's an amazing piece of sustainability.

In another case, a regional manager focused partnership formation on the state level to take advantage of the state's focus on physical activity minutes during the school day:

> *I submitted a proposal to the Office of State Superintendent of Education, which invests quite heavily into [the school district] for . . . the creation of a recess coach position. . . . This entity is really focused on helping schools to meet the Healthy Schools Act requirement with regards to PE and physical activity minutes. Last year they made a $10 million investment on the PE side. They want to focus on physical activity this year, so I'm hoping that their investment will be equal or somewhat substantial.*

The investment by the state into PE programs was significant, and by leveraging the existing statewide initiative, this regional leader was trying to put recess on the map as an essential component of a healthy school.

Recess reforms can also happen without district- or state-level support if a recess champion at the school is committed to seeing the reforms through until they are embedded in practice. This process could take several years, so it is important that not just one person be committed to making the most of recess time for children. This recess champion (referred to as a manager in this quote) is essential for moving forward, according to this regional Playworks program manager:

> *I think the biggest strength of a school that does well is having a strong recess manager. At most of the schools the recess manager is an assistant principal. If they make that a priority or something that's important to them, then the program seems to be going well.*

The champion is the person who leads the effort to remake recess and puts together a team of supporters, including the on-the-ground person who leads recess every day, the recess coach.

The Role of the Recess Coach

The steps required to organize recess at a school are relatively straightforward, but they do require a person on the ground who can implement the play yard changes, negotiate for support, and work day to day with students, recess monitors, and administrators to negotiate change and facilitate play. Like every winning team, recess needs a great coach. This person implements the steps to organize recess so that it promotes students' physical, social, and emotional development; reduces conflict; and supports students as they have fun. In most cases, the recess champion should not also be the recess coach. A champion needs a coach to help execute the reforms, and a coach needs a champion to help secure resources or amend rules and policies to support a better functioning recess.

Principal Russo in Richard Babbitt Elementary had previously looked at other recess reforms that could help her to organize activities for students to increase engagement and decrease behavioral problems. She found these reforms to be challenging for her personally because she would be the one to invest her limited time into making sure staff and students were doing what they were supposed to do to support the recess reform effort. She did not have someone to delegate this work to, and for Principal Russo, this made those reforms impossible. With Playworks, an external person—the coach—took care of the day-to-day oversight, and Principal Russo felt this was an initiative she could support:

> And, actually, [a recess coach] takes the pressure off... *any other* [organized] recess program. The principal's still responsible for monitoring the aides and having the assistants and aides out in the yard, standing by their station, doing this, doing that. But because he uses junior coaches and he doesn't really infringe upon their lunchroom duties—which do include recess, which they don't like, I mean, the older... the aides don't like doing recess, you have to get out and move around. They don't like doing that; they like to stand around and talk.... They don't quite know how to play with the kids.... So, that was a burden on me for other recess programs.

Not every school will be able to afford a full-time coach like the one Principal Russo had, but even a part-time paraprofessional coach to work in tandem with the recess champion will go a long way toward making progress in recess reform. Recess coaches like these were employed in the

TeamUp program and for the most part were members of the recess team already, but then were given an additional set of responsibilities, like Coach Diana from Northside Elementary. Coach Diana had been a member of the school's recess supervisory team when she was promoted to recess coach and supported by her principal to make changes that would engage more students in play at recess.

Other schools chose professional staff instead of paraprofessionals because of their more rigorous training and experience working with students. For example, one school relied on the school counselor to act as a recess coach because the counselor knew the students, knew how to engage with them supportively, and could be a strong support for modeling prosocial behavior. The biggest problem was that the school counselor had other responsibilities that sometimes took place during recess, which meant she was not available to coach. A regional Playworks manager described the problem as follows:

> *Our new school [is] a little bit different because they refuse to select a noon-time aide to run the program. We've talked to them all year, and they just won't pick someone who's outside every day. They're using their school counselor. And through no fault of her own, she just can't be outside every time. . . . We . . . could use someone else out there. . . . Without a solid person outside, it just isn't taking shape how we like it to.*

Another school chose to use the PE teacher as the recess coach and had the same problem: "Through no fault of his own, he just might not be able to be outside every day."

There are certainly trade-offs between having a professional and a paraprofessional recess coach. Professionals are trained already and likely have the skills either in social and emotional learning or in leading games and activities, or both. But they are busy and may have multiple obligations that may take precedence during recess time. Paraprofessionals are not as well trained, or trained at all, but if being recess coach is their only job during recess, they are likely to be able to stay in their post and support recess as needed. With some training and ongoing support, a paraprofessional who likes to engage with children can be an excellent recess coach and will be able to partner with the recess champion to bring about important changes to the recess culture.

How Can Schools and School Districts Support Recess Staffing?

The two key supports needed from a staffing perspective are (1) a paid position that is devoted to supporting recess (the coach) and (2) release time for recess coaches during their normal working hours or pay for working additional hours to participate in capacity building. The combination of these two will help the recess reform to go more smoothly.

Most schools and school districts do not have the position "recess coach" in their human resources directories. The recess coach (supervisor, aide, or whatever else you might want to name it) is the person who is in charge of the play yard and recess activities on a day-to-day basis. This person plans the activities, ensures adequate equipment is available, spearheads the effort to promote conflict resolution and a supportive recess environment, plays with students, and sets the tone for recess every day.

This coach may be the only person in the entire school to interact with every student every single day, and as such it is an important position to create and fill. Most schools do have recess supervisors (yard monitors, yard duties, lunch aides), who are generally hired under other categories and often hold more than one role at school—for instance, as an instructional aide and a yard monitor. Finding a recess coach who is qualified for the job requires a job description that matches the responsibilities of the person to be hired. These job descriptions are often the purview of the school district, which is responsible for human resources, and so an important role the district can play to support recess reforms is to create a job description that matches the job of recess coach. Working with schools to determine what are the roles and responsibilities of recess coach and to create a position tailored to those needs is an essential first step. Funding a new recess coach position while maintaining yard supervisors who are tasked with ensuring student safety would also be extremely helpful for schools.

If the recess coach role is to be filled by a paraprofessional, that person will need training or capacity-building opportunities to ensure he or she is ready for the task. Even existing yard monitors who become recess coaches

> **Recess coach job duties**
>
> - Plan daily recess, including game offerings for different age groups.
> - Engage a group of up to fifty students per recess period.
> - Implement strategies to maintain student safety, security, and well-being.
> - Implement, support, and play games with students.
> - Model inclusion, good sportsmanship, and conflict resolution practices.
> - Manage and organize equipment for activities.
> - Develop strong relationships with students and school staff.

may need capacity building to help them rethink their job at recess and learn to how connect with students through play. Recess coaches can go to a number of places for capacity building and training. One is Playworks, which has a variety of options for training that vary in cost. Other options include Peaceful Playgrounds, which has training in a variety of topic areas including bullying prevention or using the materials designed by the Centers for Disease Control and Prevention and SHAPE America for rethinking recess from a positive youth development perspective.[13] Regardless of where this capacity building comes, providing release time for recess coaches and other recess staff members during their work day to participate in training, even though they are typically part-time positions, is an important way to ensure that the goals of recess are met. If release time during the school day cannot be arranged, paying for their hours of training is essential to making sure they are up to the important tasks ahead.

Scheduling and Staffing for Effective Recess Reform

Whether lunch should come before or after midday recess, whether students of different ages should be scheduled to play together, and what combination of professional and paraprofessional staffing should support recess factor in to the reform efforts. These seemingly mundane decisions about human resources and scheduling can have large repercussions for how students experience recess and whether they are able to use that time to learn and grow outside the classroom. The underlying backbone to the success of any recess reform effort is assessing and changing local policy and staffing to support organized recess.

CHAPTER SEVEN

Improving State and Federal Recess Policies

In the late 1980s and 1990s when the standards-based accountability movement in education had taken hold, leaving recess on the sidelines in favor of more instructional time, another trend was also on the rise. Childhood obesity rates had begun to inch up during the 1970s, but by the late 1980s and 1990s, there was a skyrocketing increase, leading to what was seen by the turn of the century as a childhood obesity epidemic. In 2004, nearly one-fifth of elementary-aged children were obese, more than four times higher than the rate for the same age group in the early 1970s.[1] In that same year, a panel of experts commissioned by the National Academies' Institute of Medicine put together a set of recommendations focused on mechanisms for supporting healthy behaviors that were intended to slow the epidemic. In a *New York Times* article that fall, Dr. Jeffrey Koplan, who chaired the expert panel, remarked that their goal was to reframe the problem from an individual one to an environmental one, stating, "I think we need to make a revolution in our society. What we found with other health matters—fluoridation, bicycle helmets, smoking—is that you develop societal changes and then there is a shift in what is societally acceptable."[2] Mechanisms for creating this societal change can take many forms, including changes to federal, state, and local policies.

Indeed, as I will explore in this chapter, changes to policies and guidelines about physical activity in schools and at recess time did result from this epidemic. With regard to recess specifically, however, these changes were limited by the single-minded view that recess is a vehicle for physical activity at school. While physical activity can be one benefit of recess, other benefits accrue from a well-executed recess, including improved attention and behavior in class, social and emotional growth, and enhanced overall school climate, all of which are positively associated with academic achievement. Without acknowledgment of these multiple benefits and attention to creating the conditions for nurturing them, policy will fall short.

Today's federal legislation includes as its only recess policy the basic recommendations that schools schedule recess before lunch and incorporate physical activity into indoor and outdoor recess time. Most education policy is made at the state level, but robust recess policies are also not present in the majority of states. Where state policies associated with recess exist, they tend to focus on ensuring a certain number of physical activity minutes are met, either through recess or other mechanisms. Not one of the policies or guidelines at the state or federal levels addresses the multiple goals of recess or the necessary inputs that go into a well-designed and executed recess, including any staffing or resources needed to support it. Not until 2016, when the Centers for Disease Control and Prevention and SHAPE America released their own guidance on recess—informed by a diverse set of school-based and health-based stakeholders—did we see a whole child focus and an acknowledgment that simply scheduling recess does not ensure that physical activity will ensue. These are guidelines and not mandates, however, and therefore do not necessitate any change to the status quo.

Although thus far policy has fallen short in creating the reforms needed to ensure equitable access to recess and provisions that support the multiple ways recess time buoys child development, nevertheless, policy is a key lever for change and must be addressed for large-scale improvements in recess to occur. In this chapter, I discuss what state and federal legislation has addressed in terms of recess, what more policy could address, and what information we need to gather to ensure equitable access to recess.

Federal Policy and Guidance

The federal government has played a relatively small role in governing recess time. Although some federal legislation does include provisions that touch on recess, the US Department of Education has no recess policies or guidelines. As is discussed in this section, recess can be regulated through other mechanisms, for instance, local school wellness policies. However, guidance for these policies does not consider recess as part of a whole child approach, instead focusing on it solely as a vehicle for increasing physical activity, which restricts its vision and treatment in policy. The newest set of federal recess recommendations comes from the Centers for Disease Control and Prevention, which for the first time considers recess policy through a new and more holistic lens.

Local School Wellness Policies

The federal government responded to the National Academies' Institute of Medicine recommendations by including, as part of the 2004 Child Nutrition and Special Supplemental Nutrition Program for Women, Infants, and Children Reauthorization Act, a provision enacting local school wellness policies for the first time. Further refined in 2014 with a provision in the Healthy, Hunger-Free Kids Act of 2010, today all local education agencies that offer free and reduced-price lunch or breakfast programs are required to create these wellness policies.[3] A local school wellness policy is a document framed by school districts or other local educational agencies that outlines policies to promote students' health, well-being, and ability to learn by supporting healthy eating and physical activity.[4] Each local school wellness policy must address a set of required components, but recess falls under a nonspecific component focused on physical activity as a way to promote wellness.[5] By subsuming it within the broader physical activity parameters, recess is diminished to just another place for exercise.

Even as a place for physical activity, guidance for the treatment of recess in local school wellness policies is inadequate because there are not

> **Required elements for local school wellness policies**
> - goals for nutrition promotion and education
> - goals for physical activity and other school-based activities that promote student wellness
> - nutrition guidelines for foods and beverages available at school
> - agreements to engage stakeholders (parents, students, teachers, school board members, etc.) to participate in wellness policy development and implementation as well as update them regularly
> - plans to report and measure on the wellness policy implementation
> - designation of district and/or school officials responsible for ensuring school-level compliance with the wellness policy

recommendations that recess be scheduled every day or how many minutes of recess time should be included. There is also not information about what other factors would go into a wellness-promoting or even a physically active recess, such as adequately trained staff, appropriate equipment, and safe play areas. The guidance makes the flawed assumption that physical activity will ensue if recess is merely offered. As has been demonstrated throughout this book, without attention to organizing recess, many children will not be physically active or engaged in any games or sports at recess.

The guidelines for school wellness policies are unclear on what "wellness" means, making it challenging to create meaningful policies. The guidelines, however, do have language regarding physical activity and nutrition, so school district leaders responsible for overseeing the wellness policy design and implementation could very easily mistake wellness to mean only physical health. In 2004 when these policies were first put in place, they were in direct response to the obesity epidemic plaguing the nation's children and youth. With the ensuing leveling of the obesity crisis and schools' expanded focus on social and emotional learning, today wellness could take on many forms.

Analyses of wellness policies throughout the country make clear that their provisions for recess are weak. Using criteria for understanding both the comprehensiveness and strength of wellness policies as they pertain to physical activity, studies have concluded that although the criteria have been met in letter, policies lack specificity—such as the number of required minutes of physical activity—and do not include necessary elements to indicate an effective implementation.[6] These limitations also detract from creativity in any new guidance about how to improve recess; in the most recent comprehensive assessment of local school wellness policies, the only two recommendations for recess were to place it before lunch and to require it daily.[7] Again, these recommendations do not mention the many supports that go along with time allocation to ensure an accessible and developmentally appropriate recess.

These shortcomings are problematic because recess is included as a time for physical activity but is not a required element for the physical activity category. Wellness policies can meet their criteria for physical activity through physical education programs or other means, without ever attending to a need for student breaks during their academic instruction. In addition, by conceptualizing recess only as a time for physical activity, and not a time to promote other aspects of wellness, school wellness policies fall short. Taking breaks for the purpose of rest or reset is also an important aspect of wellness. And the social and emotional learning that is proven to happen at recess is similarly a key to wellness that these policies overlook entirely.

In short, legislation authorizing school wellness policies is sufficiently vague as to obscure the important benefits of recess above and beyond its opportunities for physical activity. Consequently, the policies themselves fall short on how recess can be used to promote many different aspects of student wellness. I suggest rewriting the local school wellness policy guidance so that it requires schools to address recess as its own category, rather than subsumed under physical activity. In addition, the guidance should address specific aspects of recess, including universal daily recess, social and emotional learning, and the need to offer more than a single break in formal learning each day.

Other Federal Guidance

Other than this legislation authorizing local school wellness policies, no federal policy addresses recess. In fact, the federal government offers very little guidance about what recess could or should include. For instance, the

US Department of Education has no information on its website regarding governance for recess time. The President's Council on Sports, Fitness and Nutrition, overseen and appointed by the president, encourages youth physical activity and health, but without mention of recess. Instead, it is focused mainly on promoting youth sports participation in out-of-school settings. For many years the White House has promoted the Presidential Youth Fitness Program, which includes a physical fitness assessment that students can take in school as well as other educational materials for individuals to use in making healthy lifestyle changes. Although there are implications of the Council and the Youth Fitness Program for recess policy and practice, neither makes the connection to recess specifically in print or online materials. Even the US Report Card on Physical Activity for Children and Youth omits recess in its coverage of physical activity, focusing exclusively on high school students and extracurricular sports participation.[8]

CDC Recess Recommendations

In 2016, the federal government offered its first set of real recommendations for recess policy and practice. Moving beyond the idea that recess is just a time for physical activity, the CDC, along with SHAPE America, created a more robust and well-rounded set of guidelines for recess that align with the findings and recommendations from the research literature. The guidelines address issues such as supervision and safety in addition to physical activity, an important move because it was the first time a federal agency connected school climate and social and emotional learning to recess time.[9]

I strongly support these recommendations and hope that state and local policy makers take note and implement them. However, because they are only recommendations, states and localities are not required to address them at all. And without more specificity as to which agency should own which recommendation, it could be easy to pass the buck. All of these recommendations could be legislated at the state level but could also be used as a template to establish local board resolutions or other binding policy. It remains to be seen whether states and districts do adopt these recommendations and to what effect, but as is discussed later in this chapter, mechanisms for tracking any changes in policy are also sorely lacking.

> **Recess recommendations provided by the CDC and SHAPE America**
>
> - Prohibit the replacement of physical education with recess or using recess to meet time requirements for physical education policies.
> - Provide schools and students with adequate spaces, facilities, equipment, and supplies for recess.
> - Ensure that spaces and facilities for recess meet or exceed recommended safety standards.
> - Prohibit the exclusion of students from recess for disciplinary reasons or academic performance in the classroom.
> - Prohibit the use of physical activity during recess as punishment.
> - Provide recess before lunch.
> - Provide staff members who lead or supervise recess with ongoing professional development.

The vacuum of enforceable recess policy serves to perpetuate existing inequalities in recess that disadvantage students in low-income neighborhoods and in schools that serve high concentrations of underrepresented minority students. Because recess is central to promoting healthy development in all developmental domains—physical, intellectual, social, and emotional—it is inextricably part of a whole child education. The lack of attention to recess in federal policy must be rectified to ensure equitable access to high-quality recess that supports not only physical health but also social and emotional learning and positive school climate.

State Legislation Governing Recess

Education is notoriously governed at the state level, so one might expect that recess policies would be addressed at the state level, but unfortunately this is also not the case. In 2016, when the CDC and SHAPE America published their recess policy report and planning guides, they provided a state-by-state synopsis of laws pertaining to school-based physical activity and recess. SHAPE America surveyed state education administrators about their policies regarding physical activity and created a fact sheet for each state that is available online.[10] I have reviewed these fact sheets and identified several ways that states can and do support recess through state policies.

State Policy on Whether and How Much Recess Is Required

In 2016, eight states nationwide had policies that governed the provision of recess to elementary schools, and fifteen had policies that required a certain number of physical activity minutes during the school day (see figure 7.1). In contrast, all but one state (Iowa) had at least some standards adopted for physical education, even if schools were not required to comply. These decisions are left entirely to state education departments, with little or no oversight or guidance from the federal government.

The most common way that states address recess in their policies is indirectly through the requirement for a certain number of minutes of student opportunities for physical activity each week or month (fifteen states; see figure 7.1). For example, both Arkansas and South Carolina require a minimum of 90 minutes of physical activity per week for elementary students, in addition to 60 minutes of physical education class for a total of 150 minutes. The policies do not specify that these 90 minutes must be spent at recess, but one of the ways students can accrue the minutes is through daily scheduled recess. Colorado similarly requires the same 150 physical activity minutes but does not specify how many of those are to occur in physical education class and how many at other times during the day. Other states require fewer minutes for physical activity, for instance, 60 per week, or daily minutes (most commonly 20–30), but again these are not linked to recess. These policies do not explicitly require recess periods in schools and sometimes do not even mention recess as an option for physical activity, but nevertheless, the implications for a need to schedule recess are inherent. Because these provisions focus specifically on physical activity, they attend more to helping students to accrue the 60 minutes per day of moderate-to-vigorous physical activity than supporting an engaged and well-run recess and the multiple developmental outcomes that can result.

A set of states does explicitly require recess. As of the SHAPE America data collection in 2016, eight states require daily recess to be provided to elementary students, and five of them specify a minimum number of

FIGURE 7.1 2016 state requirements for recess and physical activity minutes (fifty states plus Washington, DC)

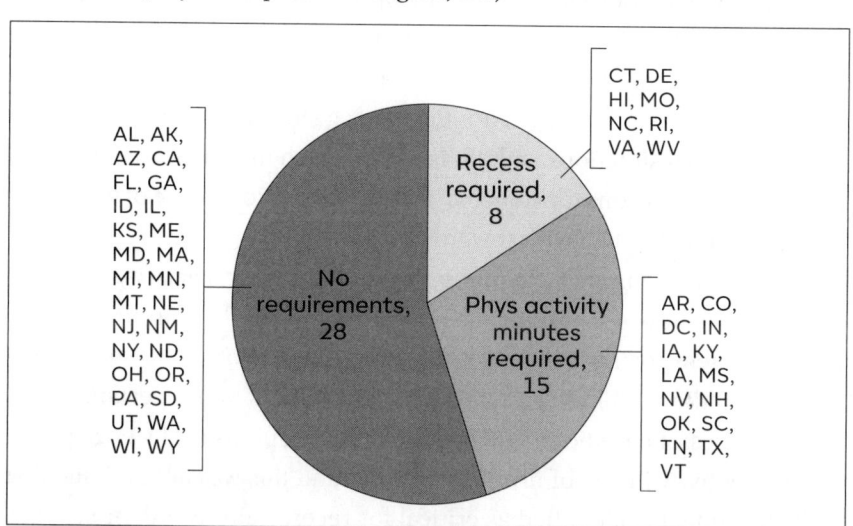

Source: CDC and SHAPE America state policy briefs available at https://www.shapeamerica.org/advocacy/advocacyresources_state.aspx

minutes (either 20 or 30). The other three do not specify minutes, but in one case policy states that the daily recess must combine with physical education to sum to 150 minutes per week. One state encourages daily recess but does not require it or provide a specified number of minutes.

Combined, there are twenty-four states (including Washington, DC) that implicitly or explicitly tackle the issue of daily recess. However, in all cases these are framed through a lens of physical activity minutes intended to address the physical health needs of children. While recess may accomplish other goals, state policies do not include guidance or requirements for what should happen to support physical activity or other developmental outcomes during that time.

The Need to Delink Discipline and Physical Activity

The CDC and SHAPE America survey asked state education administrators about two different ways that states could delink school discipline and student physical activity. The first is through prohibiting the use of denying physical activity for disciplinary purposes, including withholding recess from students as punishment. The practice of withholding recess for disciplinary purposes blocks not only opportunities for physical activity but also opportunities for social and emotional growth that may be key to students' future self-regulation and hence improved behavior. In addition, repeated recess withholding sends the message to children that they do not belong in social situations with their peers, which in and of itself can have negative repercussions for students' identity formation, sense of belonging at school, and their behavior toward others.

The second is through prohibiting the use of physical activity for disciplinary purposes—for instance, having children run laps around a track as punishment for misbehavior. This policy does not relate specifically to recess although physical activity as punishment could certainly take place at recess. I have no record of students being punished by engaging in physical activity in any of my observations, and this was not an issue that study respondents identified as critical for recess culture at their schools. Still, using physical activity as punishment can run counter to the goal of embedding positive wellness habits for children at a young age if they associate exercise with punishment.

Among the twenty-three states that have recess or physical activity minutes policies, ten also have policies aimed at delinking physical activity from punishment. In addition, four states that are not among the twenty-three also have one or both of these policies. Figure 7.2 depicts the combinations of policies that states have in place.

A total of nine states have policies that prohibit withholding recess as punishment for disciplinary purposes, and they are spread across states that have recess required, states that have physical activity minute requirements, and those with neither. Twelve states have policies that prohibit using physical activity as punishment for misbehavior. This policy is tangential to recess because this punishment could take place at any time during the day, but it's worth noting that more states disallow physical activity for punishment than disallow withholding recess for punishment. The majority of states have no policies that delink physical activity from discipline, as the majority of states also have no requirements for recess and/or physical activity minutes.

FIGURE 7.2 2016 state policies for recess, physical activity, and delinking physical activity from punishment (fifty states plus Washington, DC)

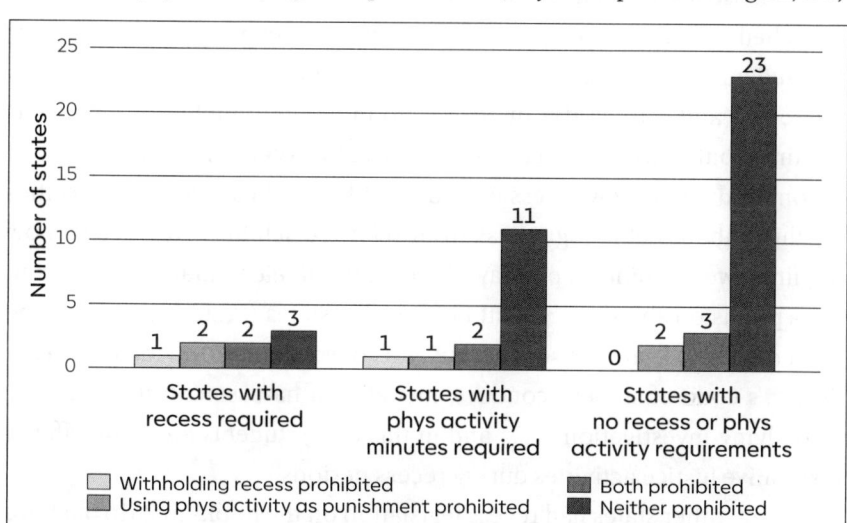

Source: CDC and SHAPE America state policy briefs available at https://www.shapeamerica.org/advocacy/advocacyresources_state.aspx

Clearly, there is still a long way to go in legislating the basic tenets of a universally accessible recess: scheduling recess for every child every day and ensuring that recess is not withheld from children for punishment purposes. Only three states nationwide had the combination of these two policies in place in 2016, according to the CDC/SHAPE America survey. Much more can and should be done by state legislation to support recess in schools.

What's New in State Policy?

In the time since 2016, when these state legislative reports were published, a few changes have been made to state recess legislation, with more states passing new laws where none existed, and others updating their existing laws that govern recess. For example, Arizona, Florida, and New Jersey all had no recess policy in 2016 at the time of the survey, but subsequently, each has legislated recess. In Florida, 2017 legislation specifies that all children in kindergarten through fifth grade must have a consecutive twenty-minute recess every day (although charter schools are exempted from the requirement).[11] This recess can take place either outdoors or indoors, and local districts are given the authority to determine how and when these are scheduled. In Arizona, schools must provide two daily recess periods for students in kindergarten through third grade, and this will expand to the fourth and fifth grades in 2019.[12] No minimum number of minutes is required, but schools are also not required to expand their school day to accommodate the new recess periods. Neither of these new laws specifies anything about delinking recess from school discipline. New Jersey now requires twenty minutes per day of recess for all elementary students and has a provision about recess withholding that states, "A student shall not be denied recess for any reason, except as a consequence of a violation of the district's code of student conduct, including a harassment, intimidation, or bullying investigation ... ," and in this case, students are to be offered restorative justice activities during recess periods.[13]

Several other states had recess legislation on the books in 2016 but have since revised them. In Rhode Island, previous law specified that recess was required but did not offer a number of minimum daily or weekly minutes. New legislation from 2016 specifies that students must have twenty consecutive minutes of daily recess. Advocates had hoped for a clause that prohibits withholding recess as punishment, but instead the legislation only recommends that recess not be withheld.[14] Note the use of the phrase "free play" in the text of the legislation shown on the next page, designating recess as a time that should not be structured, as is the case with a physical education class. Organized recess would be considered free play for the purposes of this legislation. In legislating the number of minutes, Rhode Island introduced another recess support in its legislation that other states are also beginning to employ.[15] It explicitly allows schools to count recess as instructional time so that they do not need to extend the school day to meet the daily requirement.

An even more detailed approach was legislated in Virginia in 2017. There, new state law allows up to 15 percent of the required 5.5 hours of daily instructional time to be used for recess (fifty minutes), effectively reducing the required minutes for core academic instruction.[16] Tennessee had previously legislated mandatory free play blocks but revised this in the 2017 session to allow for structured physical activity breaks as well.[17]

> **Text of the 2016 Rhode Island free-play recess legislation**
>
> 16-22-4.2. Free-play recess. — All children attending public schools, or any other schools managed or controlled by the state, that have elementary grades kindergarten through six (6) shall receive in those schools at least twenty (20) consecutive minutes of supervised, safe, and unstructured free-play recess each day. Free-play recess may be considered instructional time for those schools that would be required to extend the current school day in order to meet this requirement. Teachers shall make a good-faith effort to not withhold recess for punitive reasons. Free-play recess is in addition to the requirements set forth in §16-22-4. As used herein, the term "free play" means an unstructured environment, but which is supervised by appropriate school personnel or staff.

State policy is moving quickly with more and more states opting into mandatory minutes for recess time. What happens during these minutes, however, is left entirely to local districts and schools to decide. No new funds are allocated for equipment or personnel, and few provisions are put into place to ensure schools offer the mandated breaks equitably and students access them daily, as is prescribed in law. Hence, even in the minority of states where it exists, state recess policy continues to fall short in key ways that would support equitable access to developmentally appropriate recess time for all children.

Improving Documentation of Existing Recess Policies and Practices

A first step in changing recess policy and practice is to document the current landscape of recess so that local stakeholders, like a parent or principal, can see how local policy and practice compares statewide or nationwide. This important information is not available anywhere in consolidated form. Likewise, no mechanisms are currently in place for tracking the types of state or local policies enacted to govern recess, whether and how much recess schools build into their bell schedules, the student and neighborhood characteristics of schools that provide varying amounts of recess, school policies about withholding recess, and the background characteristics of students who have recess withheld for punishment.

One way to collect more information on school and district practices is to amend the guidelines for local school wellness policies to add recess as its own category, rather than subsumed as a possible subcategory to physical activity. By requiring each school to document its recess protocols, including how many minutes of recess are built into their bell schedules and school policies on withholding recess, parents, advocates, educators, and policy makers can keep track of access to recess and any disparities in access based on race/ethnicity, socioeconomic status, or other factors. The local school wellness policy is a good first step for creating incentives for schools to think about recess access specifically and to consider the role of recess in supporting multiple wellness goals in addition to physical activity.

A second way to keep track of recess policies more comprehensively is through the School Health Policies and Practices Study (SHPPS) conducted by the CDC. First implemented in 1994, the SHPPS has been administered at the state, district, school, and even classroom level, collecting information about a range of school health topics, including detailed information about recess practices (in some years). Starting in 2012, it has been administered biannually, with each administration covering a different measure of these levels. Several limitations to this study make it difficult for tracking access to recess. First, the most recent survey administration in 2016 focused only on district policies and practices, the one before it in 2014 focused on school and classroom policies and practices, and before that in 2012, it was state and district policies and practices. It is unclear what questions will be asked in which surveys.

Furthermore, the survey results are reported on the CDC website in aggregate, meaning that the general public has no way of knowing from this data collection whether schools in low-income areas or urban areas, for instance, offer recess or as many recess minutes as those in more middle-class and suburban areas. Databases are available to download and analyze, but doing so requires sophistication in data analysis that many recess observers might lack. The SHPPS is also conducted among a sample of respondents. For instance, in 2016 when the survey focused on school districts, it used a stratified random sample intended to represent the United States as a whole. However, for monitoring the state of recess, a sample is inadequate. It does not offer information to local stakeholders about their own school's or district's policies and practices. It also does not allow for direct comparison to other schools, counties, or states that could be helpful in crafting new policies or practices. However, its greatest limitation is its uncertainty in terms of whether and when it will be next offered and what data collections will be included. The 2016 reporting makes clear that there is no known plan for future administrations.[18]

A third option for collecting more information about school recess policies and practices is the Office for Civil Rights in the US Department of Education. Each year, every school and district in the United States is required to report to the Office of Civil Rights information on school programs and policies, student disciplinary actions, staffing, and other matters.[19] Each school is also required to report its student demographic breakdown so that the data can be used to explore disparities in access to educational programs, like Advanced Placement courses, and inequities in the use of disciplinary measures, such as school suspensions and expulsions. The Office of Civil Rights data collection asks no questions about recess or physical activity and no questions about opportunities for social and emotional learning.

Throughout this book I've demonstrated that recess and access to it are substantively a civil right and a human right. The Office of Civil Rights should add to its existing data collections information about how many minutes of recess are scheduled per day, policies about withholding recess, and programs in place to support recess as a time for social and emotional learning. This kind of transparency would provide academics, policy makers, educators, and parents the information they need to assure recess can be accessed by everyone.

Moving Forward in Federal and State Policy and Practice

Although state policy has come a long way in just the past few years with more and more states beginning to legislate requirements for recess in elementary schools, much more can be done. The two policy mechanisms that have been used thus far for governing recess are inadequate to ensure equitable access to productive recess for every child. At the federal level, the requirement for local school wellness policies does not go nearly far enough toward setting the conditions for a high-quality recess, and furthermore, the wellness policies are unenforceable. At the state level, many states have no legislation or guidelines that govern the availability of recess or the number of required minutes. Large states such as California are among those that have not addressed this issue. Like other instructional time, recess should be required for all students every day, and if this requirement is not put into policy by state educational leaders and legislators, there is no guarantee of equitable access to recess. Some states have used state legislation to address limited aspects of recess, and many states have done nothing at all. More can be done in both arenas to aid school districts and schools to support students getting the most out of their recess time, not only offering physical exercise but also meeting their social and emotional needs.

It is important to note that state and federal policy cover only public schools. The local school wellness policies are further limited to public schools that offer a free and reduced-price meal program. To really create equitable access to recess, all schools—whether public or private, and including charter schools—should be part of the policy reforms.

Three key limitations associated with the policy approaches have been taken thus far. First, policy levers have been motivated by a vision of recess solely as a location for physical activity. Messaging from the public health industry has been effective in advocating for mandated recess and even a certain number of minutes. This is a huge victory, and I am personally excited to see it happen. However, much is lost in a vision of recess as only a place for physical activity. Although it is certainly a time when children are active, it is also, as this book has shown, a time for learning in other developmental areas, for socializing, and for taking a break from the structure of the classroom. If one could think about recess legislation in a tiered system, tier 1 might be making sure it happens for every child every day, and tier 2 could be making sure it happens for every child every day for a certain number of minutes. Tier 2 policies might also include provisions about prohibiting the withholding of recess for disciplinary issues and allowing recess to count toward instructional minutes, which removes disincentives from offering it. Anything beyond tier 2 is not even an option in today's state policy landscape, but imagine tier 3 policies that might add a quality matrix to ensure that criteria for recess implementation—in terms of safety, facilities, and supervision, for instance—are met. We have not yet seen policies or guidelines that discuss the qualifications of recess monitors or any required credentialing or professional development that could be applied to these positions. Nor have we seen funding allocations to ensure equitable access to recess. As far as I know, no state has provided curricular guidance or a set of standards to be met for recess time. The research literature falls short in this area as well, and more scholarly work could be done to support the creation of recess standards.

A second limitation with existing approaches is the underlying assumption that providing recess and even specific minutes for recess will increase physical activity or the opportunity for physical activity for all students. As this book has demonstrated, this assumption is unfounded. The most active students who desperately want to play sports at recess will find a way to do that if given the space. For the rest of the student population, being herded outside to play for twenty minutes cannot be translated into twenty minutes of moderate-to-vigorous physical activity. There are many reasons for this, but to select a few that I mentioned in prior chapters of this book: (1) yard supervisors will keep students waiting in line until they are absolutely still before releasing them to play, (2) lack of appropriate equipment and space limit physical activity and play, (3) games are exclusive and not open to all students, (4) supervision does not encourage active play, and so on. State policy also does not address how physical activity minutes are to be accrued when bad weather precludes outdoor recess. It is not necessarily the role of state policy to govern these local aspects of recess, but ignoring the role of local practices is also problematic. Attending to how recess functions is the best way to ensure students are physically active during this time. This is a place where local school wellness policies could be more specific, particularly if recess were given its own category in the required components. A great template is the CDC/SHAPE America recommendations, which address local practice in several areas, including providing adequate facilities and equipment, ensuring safety standards are met, and providing ongoing professional development to staff who supervise recess.[20]

The third limitation of existing policies is that they are unfunded mandates. If we want to see change during recess time, we must be willing to allocate resources and create systems of support. Simply having a policy that says recess is mandated is insufficient to create an engaged recess experience for students. As with any instructional time, planning, professional development, and instructional materials all go into a successful effort. And for recess, currently no funding is attached to the new policies.

Using existing federal and state policy mechanisms can improve access to recess and, importantly, ensure recess is provided more equitably so that all students have the chance for a break in the school day. Becoming a recess champion in a local school or district is one way to ensure that students in your local area are getting the best recess they can. But to assure that access to high-quality recess is universal, state and federal policy mechanisms and measurement must improve.

CHAPTER EIGHT

The Right to Play

Elementary school recess is more than just a short break for students to run around and let off some steam. With planning and coordination, recess is an opportunity for students to learn and practice important social and emotional skills, to support classroom-based character development and climate programs in other school-based settings, and to have a refocusing break with a chance to be physically active. Now is the time for educators and policy makers to recognize the critical role of recess in schools and support changes to improve its potential for supporting "whole child" development and positive school climate.

A history of excluding recess from the school day in favor of more academic learning time—a misguided approach thought to improve standardized test scores—is in the process of being reversed. Today, the pendulum of thinking on the role of recess in school is beginning to swing, and many of the school districts that had previously cancelled recess have now reinstated it. States have passed or are considering legislation to require recess as an essential part of the school day for elementary students. In addition, the practice of withholding recess as punishment for misbehavior or missed schoolwork is starting to be addressed in policy, recognizing it as harmful to children and counterproductive to the goals of healthy child development. Research presented in this book supports both of these changes and advocates for policies that ensure daily recess for every elementary child as a basic human right. Yet requiring access alone is not a guarantee that recess will be a positive developmental experience for children. To generate the maximum impact of this short but important part of the school day, recess must be designed with consideration for student needs, integrated with existing school initiatives, and led by committed adults with proper training to support student social, emotional, and physical growth.

A prescription for recess comes straight from the pediatrician's office, with the American Academy of Pediatrics and the Centers for Disease Control and Prevention both weighing in on the importance of recess in schools. Play, in and out of the context of recess, is so important for the development of young children that the American Academy of Pediatrics now encourages pediatricians to prescribe play to preschool-aged children, and the United Nations has designated play a fundamental right of children. Yet access to this important developmental catalyst here in the United States is not equal; students who are low income and from underrepresented minority backgrounds have less access to recess than their more advantaged and white peers. Also, it is still within the purview of most classroom teachers and lunchroom monitors to withhold recess from individual children or entire classes for any reason. It is every child's fundamental right to play, and the play that happens in the elementary school yard should be accessible to all children, regardless of where they live, their family's income, their ethnic background, or their academic abilities.

With this recess revival comes a question: what do we need to do to ensure a great recess for all children? Principals across the country report challenges with recess, such as not having recess monitors who are well trained to support children's play and lacking recess yard environments that support play in an inclusive way. Disciplinary problems are a chief concern with recess, as recess is a primary location for bullying and many schools experience a daily spike in office referrals stemming from that time. How to embed a well-thought-out and executed recess into a busy elementary school day is a challenge, and overcoming that challenge has been the focus of this book.

I have made the case for an "organized recess." An organized recess is not structured, like a physical education class with little free choice, but provides different choices for games and activities and consistent rules for playing them. Organized recess embeds options for free play but is not exclusively a free play zone. While some children may choose to engage in imaginative play, where they devise their own games that stretch their creativity, other activities are also available for students. Choice is a key to organized recess, with ample opportunities for all kinds of play, tools for resolving conflict, inclusivity, and adult support. Based on my own and others' research, I have concluded that organized recess is a common-sense path between the boundaries of free play and structured recess that offers the best opportunities to cultivate social and emotional skills, which are essential for student success. Adults have the critical role of facilitating that time. These changes can be brought about in affordable ways that maximize students' enjoyment and sense of safety at recess.

The Important Role of Organized Recess

The central argument of this book is that recess, like any other time of the school day, requires some planning. Organizing recess is not a one-size-fits-all approach but rather involves customization to incorporate the school context and students' needs in creating a recess environment that provides the greatest opportunities for student engagement and development. Schools that are reinstating recess after a hiatus can use the book as a planning guide for designing a new kind of recess that works with their students and staffing. Those that face daily recess challenges like disciplinary incidents and bullying can similarly assess and plan with those specific problems in mind. Schools that have a well-established recess period can also still learn, plan, and try to engage even more students in recess activities. Policy makers, educational leaders, and advocates can learn from the process I lay out to create policies and practices that support organized recess, engaging all children in safe and healthy play environments.

Creating an organized recess is a group effort but requires one person to spearhead the process—a person I call the "recess champion." Frequently, the recess champion is a school administrator, principal, or assistant principal who has heard about or seen recess reform in action in another school and attempts that same process in his or her own school. The champion does not have to be a school administrator, however. In my own research, I have seen school counselors, physical education teachers, and even a school nurse take up the mantle of recess champion. All it takes is a commitment to reforming recess and an ability to provide or harness the support of top administrators for the process. Often, a recess champion will self-identify, but if not, someone can be recruited and supported to fill this position, which is the cornerstone of the reform effort.

With a recess champion in place, the next steps can be done by a team of interested stakeholders, which could include administrators, teachers, parents, recess support staff, students, and custodial staff. Different stakeholders can focus on different steps and still work toward the common goal of improving recess. The key to a successful reorganization effort is ensuring that school policies and practices support and align with the goals for recess. This effort includes offering daily recess for all children and not withholding recess to punish children for misbehavior or missed schoolwork.

Once a recess champion has been identified and empowered, this person must be supported while making the basic changes that are at the heart of recess organization. These steps are described in more detail in earlier chapters but summarized here.

STEP 1. **Assess the landscape.** Assess the recess facilities with an eye toward removing safety hazards, creating more play space, and adding features like markings for games that children like to play (e.g., four-square). *Tip: Use the Playworks' Great Recess Framework or the US Consumer Product Safety Commission's Public Playground Safety Handbook.*[1]

STEP 2. **Assess the recess policy structures at school.** Explore the recess policies in your school (or district or state), including whether recess is included in the daily bell schedule as well as policies and practices for lunch and recess scheduling and withholding recess. The goal is daily access to recess for all children. *Tip: Convene a task force including administrators, recess staff, teachers, and students to conduct this assessment and make recommendations.*

STEP 3. **Explore the play culture at school.** Observe children's play at recess to identify the games that are most popular and problematic, the groups that are most and least engaged, and the need for age-appropriate adjustments to recess game offerings. Consider introducing games that do not require equipment to minimize costs. *Tip: Partner with the physical education teacher, the city's Parks and Recreation department, or a local nonprofit like the Boys & Girls Club for ideas.*

STEP 4. **Engage in low-cost updates, if possible.** Explore low-cost updates such as adding new markings on blacktop or repaving, planting green spaces, removing hazards, or improving playground equipment. *Tip: Apply for grants, as needed, to support these efforts.*[2]

STEP 5. **Provide necessary loose equipment, if possible.** Purchase play equipment like balls, cones, and jump ropes, if necessary. *Tip: Apply for grants or share equipment with PE classes.*

STEP 6. **Centralize and systemize the equipment checkout.** Establish a central checkout system that is overseen by adults (e.g., parent volunteers or recess monitors) or students to minimize losses and maintain equipment integrity. *Tip: Embed equipment checkout as part of a recess leadership program for students.*

STEP 7. **Map the play yard with different activity zones or game locations.** Identify areas of the play yard where various games children like are consistently available, ensuring space is available for those who want to engage in their own imaginative play or have a quieter recess experience. To create spaces that do not overlap, you may need to set up weekly rotations of certain games while keeping core games available daily. *Tip: Involve students and parents in the design of the play space.*

STEP 8. **Roll out the format to adults and students.** Share the changes with all school stakeholders, starting with teachers and other school staff, and including both students and parents. Having enlisted a broad array of stakeholders in the planning process will help with the rollout phase. *Tip: Provide training for all recess monitors to support the new format.*

Rolling out the new format per step 8 can take many forms, including simply convening a school assembly to discuss the new playground rules. However, to truly optimize a high-functioning organized recess, the rollout itself must include some important changes in staffing and recess culture.

Hire, promote, and train a recess coach. A key person to identify in the recess reform effort is the recess coach, or the person who is out at recess every day and does the recess "lesson planning" as well as ensures that recess organization is in place. This coach can be anyone, but it is best for it to be someone whose job is to be at recess so that person will not be pulled away with other responsibilities that might supersede recess duty. A recess monitor or classroom aide, crossing guard, afterschool program staff, physical education teacher, or even a parent can be a recess coach.

Embed recess reform into school culture. The recess plan should be tailored to the overall school culture and climate and incorporate any existing programs for character development, social and emotional learning, or bullying prevention. This plan will look different at every school, but some features to consider are conflict resolution, inclusivity, and student leadership.

Identify and promote simple conflict resolution strategies. In an engaged play space, conflict is expected, and learning to resolve simple conflicts—like whether the ball was in or out and who goes first in a game—is an important skill that can be practiced at recess. Without a plan for how students should resolve small conflicts, they can quickly escalate into more serious altercations. If students are not prepared to start or sustain games on their own and need help with this step, a simple tool used by Playworks for conflict resolution is rock-paper-scissors. When implemented so that students know how to play the game and understand they can use it just once to resolve their simple conflict, this approach can be highly effective in promoting easy conflict resolution and sustained play. Rock-paper-scissors does not solve every problem though, and for some conflicts, students may need other tools. How they approach conflict resolution depends on the school's overall approach. Some schools use a talk-it-out approach, and others expect students to bring problems to an adult or use restorative justice practices to resolve conflicts. There is no right way to do this, but having a plan for helping students who cannot resolve conflicts on their own is important.

Create an inclusive play yard. Students who feel unwelcome to join a game will not play. Organizing recess requires a mindset change where the goal is for every child to have an opportunity for engagement, and if it is a learning space (as all school spaces are), even those with burgeoning skills in a particular game should have the option to learn and play. Having an exclusive soccer or basketball game is not aligned with this approach, and various options exist to deescalate competitive games or create options for students of all abilities to join in.

Offer student leadership opportunities. Student leaders can be brought in as early as the planning process (after all, students know what works and doesn't at recess and which games are popular). They can also play a role in ongoing support of recess in a variety of ways—for instance, by checking out equipment, being on cleanup duty, or running game stations for younger children and helping them to play by the rules. A well-executed student leadership program requires ongoing support and training for students, which is a commitment, particularly if a diverse set of student leaders is selected—including those with established leadership skills and those who may need more leadership skill development. Having student leaders can improve the overall recess experience for students as well as aid in improving the recess behaviors of the student leaders themselves.

What's Next for the Field of Recess?

While I was writing this book, the greatest challenge was a lack of consistent data on the nature and extent of recess nationwide and the policies that govern it at the local and state levels. I relied heavily on one-time data collections conducted by researchers in various locations, which typically included samples of schools or school districts rather than a census of information that parents and advocates on the local level can use to track their own region's recess policies and practices. If creating equitable access to meaningful recess is a goal worth legislating, as I suggest, then tracking how and how often recess is offered by every school nationwide is a logical next step.

Tracking recess provision fits well with the goals of the US Department of Education Office of Civil Rights' annual data collection. Currently, that office collects information about a variety of civil rights issues, including access to high-level coursework for high school students, disciplinary actions such as suspensions and expulsions, teacher qualifications, school expenditures, and student demographic characteristics. They include data on criminal offenses that occur at schools, which affect few students, but have no information at all about recess policies or practices that affect every elementary student nationwide. The Office of Civil Rights data have been essential for tracking issues like the disproportionality in disciplinary actions for African American students, and advocates have used them to call for alternatives, like restorative justice practices. If the data included information on recess policies and practices, imagine how that evidence could arm advocates with what they need to support equitable access to a high-quality recess.

I suggest that the most important items for inclusion on the Office of Civil Rights data collection are the following:

- school, district, and state policies on access to recess and any policies governing recess, such as whether recess is required and number of required minutes, lunch is to be offered after recess, and withholding recess for punishment for misbehavior or missed schoolwork is allowable
- school-level data on the how these recess policies are implemented, including number of recess periods and minutes per period, the timing of lunch and play, and the number and characteristics of students who have recess withheld (e.g., ethnicity, disability status)
- school-level data on the training provided to recess monitors
- school-level data on recess facilities, such as the size of the yard, safety concerns, and equipment available

I recommend collecting these data for all schools serving children in grades K–8. Although this book has focused exclusively on elementary schools, students in middle schools and junior high schools also have breaks for recess scheduled, and the same concerns about access and equity apply for these early adolescents. I have intentionally kept this list parsimonious, but of course much more could be collected to better understand recess operations nationwide.

Aside from data, which is key, we also need to improve the field of research on recess to better characterize its benefits and limitations, and provide evidence for what works best in different context. The limitation of nearly all the recess literature, my own studies included, is that these studies are cross-sectional, meaning they take place during one slice of time—data collections at one point in time or over one school year. I am not aware of any longitudinal recess studies that track schools over long periods of time as they make changes to their recess. Issues of sustainability in the context of changing school leadership, changing student populations, new policy regimes, and new programmatic emphases are essential. Unfortunately, research funding typically comes in two- to three-year chunks, so options for carrying on this work over longer periods are limited. However, longitudinal tracking would add to the story of recess reform in important ways and should be considered a next step for the field.

A second area in which research could be expanded is in the linking of physical and social/emotional outcomes associated with recess. At the moment, the literature tends to be split. Researchers concerned with physical activity and physical development tend to conduct experimental research that compares students at schools with various recess reforms in terms of their mobility and minutes of physical activity. These studies often do not consider the school context in great detail; many do not even describe the student population beyond their ethnic backgrounds. These studies serve to reinforce the notion that recess is an add-on to the school day and not an essential part of the learning process. By focusing solely on physical activity as the outcome, they lack the ability to help schools integrate recess better into the school day and take into account school constraints—such as low standardized test scores—that may infringe on schools' abilities to undertake reforms at recess.

The literature on social and emotional development at recess and the importance of play for young children is also, in some ways, devoid of this school context. Although these studies do describe the schools and children that are the subjects of the research, the schools are more homogeneous middle income or serve predominantly white children. The literature on play needs to be updated to include the diversity of today's schoolchildren and the various issues they face in play. For instance, how does having a limited knowledge of the English language affect play during recess, or in what ways do cultural differences in play norms affect students' play experiences in schools? These and other issues must be explored for the literature to remain current and relevant in today's school settings.

I argue that it is critical to consider the "whole child" in thinking about recess. Children's development does not parse itself into either physical or social/emotional, but rather all this development happens for students at the same time. Their experiences are shaped by both their physical and social/emotional capacities, and their development in all these areas can be aided by supportive recess policies and practices. I have attempted to consider the whole child in my own research, and others are also thinking in this way. However, as the field is currently dominated by health professionals, the policies that are being implemented are more about access to recess and minutes of recess, with an eye toward the sixty minutes of physical activity suggested by the American Academy of Pediatrics. If the field were instead focused on an understanding that the goals of social and emotional learning are best accessed at recess, we would seek to build policy and practices that served social and emotional learning goals. When we consider the whole child, practices such as organized recess, which attend to both the social/emotional and the physical development needs of children, are the logical response.

An Ounce of Prevention

A mindset shift about recess is needed. For many years, recess has been considered a frivolous time of day, just a chance to give teachers a lunch break while students can get their wiggles out. With this limited view, it is easy to understand why recess was first on the chopping block in the early standards-based accountability days and why even today recess is neglected rather than seen as an important augmentation to classroom learning. By neglecting recess as a learning period, schools end up with daily office referrals for recess misbehavior, unhappy students who are stressed during what should be their fun time, and recess monitors whose engagement styles are more prison guard than school teacher. Organizing recess in the ways I have suggested will turn this around and create a recess period in which students learn and grow—socially, emotionally, and physically—as well as get that needed break from their schoolwork.

When schools give children the tools to resolve conflicts, be empathetic, negotiate and collaborate, regulate their emotions in uncomfortable situations, and see themselves as part of a collective effort rather than just an individual, recess can be a preventive effort for future problems. Although research on recess reform has not tracked students longitudinally past elementary school, it is clear that with its supports for social and emotional learning and physical activity, well-planned and organized recess should be an important part of a system of prevention that promotes health and well-being as children grow into adolescence.

However, we currently operate in a system that is more intervention than prevention, stepping in to help children once an observable problem comes to light. For instance, at recess, children are left to themselves until a fight breaks out, and then there is intervention. Organized recess is a preventive approach; it anticipates known problems that occur and uses simple organizational changes to reduce problems and improve engagement. Creating an organized recess has been shown to reduce bullying, even though recess organization was not specifically about bullying at all. Learning, the charge of all schools, is also preventive as it is aimed at providing children with the skills and knowledge they need to be successful as adults. The learning embedded at recess time has similar aims, allowing children the time and space to practice their social and emotional skills through play. An additional benefit is that it's fun.

It's not a far leap to think about how organized recess implemented widely might change the too-often-heard stories of isolation, depression, and self-harm that plague today's adolescents. How would organized recess change the trajectory of a future school shooter whose profile includes a history of exclusion and bullying? How do intentional efforts for inclusion of all students at recess affect students' perceptions of themselves and their connection to society? As we strive to view our students more holistically,

I hope my research can contribute to a growing respect for recess as a site of learning where essential skills for future success and well-being are cultivated on the school playground.

A Vision of Great Recess for All

Coach Diana, whom I introduced in chapter 1, is a real person in a real school doing this hard work of recess reform every day. When I think about what success looks like for Coach Diana and Northside Elementary School, I see students who head out to recess each day, eager to play their favorite games with old and new friends. I see a play area that is organized with a variety of games and intentionally maximizes the useable space. Children are engaged in play, really playing and involved in their game, even if they are waiting in line for their next turn at four-square or wall ball. When conflicts arise, as they do, children have a plan for resolving them that allows the game to continue without interruption. Students come and go in games, and it's the norm to include anyone who wants to join in. Student leaders are checking out equipment and stationed at several of the most popular games to help them run smoothly. Adults at recess are stationed around the recess yard, not simply watching, but engaging with students, smiling at them, encouraging them, and even playing with them. And Coach Diana, the lynchpin of this recess, stands at the door as students walk out. She gives them a high five and greets them by name with a smile. Through her actions she reassures them that they are safe out here at recess. The space has been set up so that they can feel emotionally safe to take risks and join games where they feel less confident; the play yard is inclusive now and nobody will turn them away. Students feel physically safe from bullying and harassment; adults are engaged and will see if they are being mistreated. Coach Diana, whistle around her neck, joins the students in a round of dodgeball, to model what inclusion, conflict resolution, and good sportsmanship look like in practice. At the end of recess when Coach Diana blows her whistle, children take a knee. She blows it again, and they walk to line up where they will meet their teacher to return to class. Some are out of breath from running. Some are still singing jump-rope chants. Everyone has had a break. And nobody is fighting when their teachers arrive.

Behind this vision is a principal who supports Coach Diana with policies aimed at ensuring student access to daily recess. Teachers in this school are no longer allowed to withhold recess as punishment for misbehavior or missed schoolwork. Every child has access to recess every single day at Northside Elementary. Parents begin to notice that their children have learned new games and want to play them at home. Coach Diana comes to back-to-school night and opens the recess yard for children to play and share with their parents the games they like best. The whole school community becomes invested in having a great recess.

It does not take long for the school district leadership to learn about this transformation and for parents at other elementary schools to start to advocate for similar opportunities at their schools. The school district allocates funding for recess coaches at all its elementary schools and paid release time for them to be trained. It even creates a new job description called "recess coach," which differs from the recess and lunch monitor positions, detailing the special roles that a recess coach has in planning recess time. After an article in the local newspaper highlights the changes at Northside Elementary, a state legislator who is an education equity advocate takes up the issue in the state capitol. New legislation is passed mandating daily recess statewide and banning withholding recess as punishment, and recommendations are made for ways that existing funding streams can be allocated to support recess time.

Children at Northside Elementary are blissfully unaware that their recess fun has spurred policy change in the state capitol. They simply enjoy having a recess with choices of games to play, adults who connect with them and help them, new and old friends to see. Younger children eagerly await the start of their fourth-grade year for their first chance at the coveted junior coach role. Recess used to be the most stressful time of day for teachers, students, and staff. Now it's productive time for learning and growth, a time when everyone feels safe and welcome, when everyone can play and have fun.

APPENDIX 1

Resources for Rethinking Recess

Planning and practices for high-quality recess	CDC and SHAPE America, Strategies for Recess in Schools (https://www.shapeamerica.org/uploads/pdfs/recess/SchoolRecessStrategies.pdf)
	CDC and SHAPE America, Recess Planning in Schools (https://www.shapeamerica.org/uploads/pdfs/recess/SchoolRecessPlanning.pdf)
	SHAPE America, Recess Planning Template (https://www.shapeamerica.org/standards/guidelines/strategies_for_recess_in_schools.aspx?hkey=5a588845-900b-40e7-89bc-290557cf0c20)
Recess assessment	Playworks, Great Recess Framework—Observational Tool (https://www.greatrecessframework.org) and Appendix 2
	Playworks, Recess Checkup (https://www.recesslab.org/checkup/)
	US Consumer Product Safety Commission, Public Playground Safety Handbook (https://www.cpsc.gov/s3fs-public/325.pdf)
Ways to map the play yard	Playworks, Rejuvenate Your Playground (https://www.playworks.org/resource/rejuvenate-your-playground/)
	Playworks, Recess Lab: Mapping Boundaries video (https://www.youtube.com/watch?v=25hlJfkBbLc)
	Peaceful Playgrounds, Recess Stencils (https://peacefulplaygrounds.com/recess-stencils/)

Recess advocacy	Springboard to Active Schools, Keep Recess in Schools (https://nnphi.org/wp-content/uploads/2017/07/Recess-Data-Brief_FINALversion_071817.pdf)
	Peaceful Playgrounds, Right to Recess Campaign (https://peacefulplaygrounds.com/right-to-recess-campaign/)
Funding resources	Peaceful Playgrounds, School Playground Grants (https://peacefulplaygrounds.com/playground-and-garden-grants/)
	KaBoom, Playground Grants (https://kaboom.org/grants)
	Korkat Playground Equipment, Playground Grants and Fundraisers (http://korkat.com/playground-grants/)
	Snider Recreation, Grants for School Playground Equipment (http://cvsnider.com/playground-grants/)
	Playword, Grants Guide (https://playworld.com/grant-guide)
Games and game rules	Playworks, Game Library (https://www.playworks.org/game-library/)
	We Are Teachers, 25 Old-School Recess Games Your Students Should Be Playing Now (https://www.weareteachers.com/recess-games/)
	Wired, 30 Classic Outdoor Games for Kids (https://www.wired.com/2009/08/simpleoutdoorplay/)
	Angela Watson, 15 Fun Indoor Recess Games and Activities (https://thecornerstoneforteachers.com/15-fun-indoor-recess-games-and-activities/)
	Fun-Attic, 17 Indoor Recess Games (https://funattic.com/indoor-recess-games/)
Staff training	Peaceful Playgrounds, Playground Supervision Training (https://peacefulplaygrounds.com/playground-supervision/)
	Susannah Brackett, Active Supervision: Study Guide (https://www.sbbh.pitt.edu/files/Powerpoint%20Presentations%202524%20Spring%202010/Brackett_Susannah_Active_Supervision.pdf)
	Playworld, Recess Behavior Management (https://playworld.com/blog/recess-behavior-management/)
	Playworks, Recess Lab Try It Out (https://www.recesslab.org/resources/)
	Playworks, Staff Training and Online Learning (https://www.playworks.org/services/)
Alternatives to recess withholding	Peaceful Playgrounds, 60 Alternatives to Withholding Recess (https://peacefulplaygrounds.com/60-alternatives-to-withholding-recess/)
	Center for Science in the Public Interest, Alternative School Discipline Options to Withholding Recess (https://cspinet.org/sites/default/files/attachment/Alternative%20School%20Discipline%20Options%20to%20Withholding%20Recess.pdf)
	School Leaders Now, 6 Ways to Discipline Students Without Taking Away Recess (https://schoolleadersnow.weareteachers.com/how-to-discipline-a-child-without-taking-away-recess/)

APPENDIX 2

Great Recess Framework– Observational Tool (GRF-OT)

Designed and Validated by Playworks with William Massey, PhD[1]

School:	Playworks:	Yes / No
Date:	Rules Posted:	Yes / No
Rater:	Grade(s): Start Time: End Time:	

Circle Score for Each

1	2	3	4	Notes
(1) Safety Concerns—Hazards. Play space ≠ entire playground. Focus on proximity to where kids play.				
1. Significant safety concerns in **almost all** of the play space	2. Significant safety concerns in **a majority** of the play space	3. Significant safety concerns in **some** of the play spaces	4. The play space has **no** safety concerns.	Note specific hazards and where they exist.
(2) Boundaries: Identified with cones, chalk, paint, etc., AND must also be used.				
1. The play space has no clearly identified boundaries for games.	2. A majority of the play space does not have any game space marked.	3. The play space has many boundaries identified.	4. The play space is well marked and all game boundaries are clear.	Note any space that is marked for certain games and what they are; e.g., blacktop marked for kickball, area by school marked for hula hoops: Could have observers draw a playground schematic?

	1	2	3	4	Notes
(3) Safety Concerns—Size & Location: Look at size:kid ratio, access to busy streets, neighborhood.	1. The play space has many immediate safety concerns due to size and/or location.	2. The play space has some immediate safety concerns due to size and/or location.	3. The play space has very few immediate safety concerns due to size and/or location.	4. The play space for recess is appropriate—no immediate safety concerns.	Note areas unavailable for play; green space versus blacktop; community access points.
(4) Fixed & Unfixed Equipment: Basketball hoops DON'T count; must be allowed to use the equipment.	1. No fixed or unfixed recess equipment is available.	2. Only fixed OR only nonfixed recess equipment is available.	3. Fixed recess equipment is available, and there is limited nonfixed equipment.	4. Fixed and nonfixed recess equipment is available to support multiple games and activities.	List what fixed equipment is available for play and what unfixed equipment is available. Be as specific as possible (e.g., twenty jump ropes, four basketballs).
(5) Transitions to Recess: Look at hallways.	1. Hardly any transitions to recess from classroom are organized and smooth.	2. Few transitions to recess from classroom are organized and smooth.	3. Most transitions to recess from classroom are organized and smooth.	4. All transitions to recess from classroom are organized and smooth.	Note behaviors observed during transition to recess; note any observed rules (e.g., what were monitors telling kids?); note if you do not see full transition from inside.
(6) Supervising Adults: If class is late and teacher is recess supervisor, then mark down.	1. Hardly any supervising adults arrive on time, and for periods of time there is no adult supervision.	2. A few supervising adults arrive on time, but supervision is compromised because not enough adults are on the playground.	3. Most of the supervising adults arrive on time, but a few come out late.	4. All supervising adults arrive on time, and there are no periods of time in which students are unsupervised.	Notes: How many adults at start of recess? How many at five minutes? Ten minutes? End of recess?
(7) Student-to-Adult Ratio: Assess at ten minutes.	1. The student-to-adult ratio is more than 75:1.	2. The student-to-adult ratio is between 51:1 and 74:1.	3. The student-to-adult ratio is approximately 35:1 to 50:1.	4. The student-to-adult ratio is less than 35:1.	Notes: Were enough adults available to cover the dedicated space for recess? How many would be optimal?
(8) Variety of Organized Games: From the perspective of the child: "What can I play?"	1. Hardly any organized games and/or activities are available during recess.	2. A limited number of organized games and/or activities are available during recess, but there is limited variety.	3. A limited number of organized games and/or activities are available during recess, but there is variety.	4. A variety of organized games and/or activities are available during recess (~five to six games).	Notes: What are the games being played at recess? For each game consider: Who is playing the game (gender, race, other demographics)? Barriers to inclusion or patterns of exclusion? Open or closed? Aside from organized activities, document what children are doing.

Appendix 2

1	2	3	4	Notes
(9) Inclusiveness of Organized Games: Hard to score, so try your best.				
1. Almost all games are exclusive to certain groups by gender, ability, race, and/or age (if appropriate).	2. Some of the games are exclusive to certain groups by gender, ability, race, and/or age (if appropriate).	3. Some of the games are inclusive to certain groups by gender, ability, race, and/or age (if appropriate).	4. Almost all games are inclusive to a variety of groups by gender, ability, race, and/or age (if appropriate).	
(10) Game Initiation: Score low if all games are initiated by kids but not many kids are engaged.				
1. Hardly any games are initiated by students.	2. A few games are initiated by students.	3. Some games are initiated by students.	4. Almost all games are initiated by students.	Note what games children are initiating/playing. Take notes if this differs from anything adults try to organize/lead.
(11) Sustaining Games: Kids can rotate in and out. Score low if games are stopping and starting.				
1. Hardly any games are sustained by students.	2. A few games are sustained by students.	3. Some games are sustained by students.	4. Almost all games are sustained by students.	
(12) Free Choice During Recess: Autonomy. Mark down if kids come out late to recess or have to stand on the wall.				
1. Students have no free choice of activities to play during recess.	2. Students have limited free choice of activities to play during recess.	3. Students have some free choice of activities to play during recess.	4. Students are free to choose the activities to play during recess.	
(13) Physical Activity: Movement ≠ play				
1. Hardly any students are involved in physically active play.	2. Few students are involved in physically active play.	3. Some students are involved in physically active play.	4. Almost all students are involved in physically active play.	What are the nonactive kids doing? Describe differences between kids who are active and kids who are not.
(14) Equipment Use: Hogging equipment, using it in an unsafe manner, climbing fences. Kids can be creative with how they use equipment as long as it is safe.				
1. Hardly any equipment provided is being used as intended and in a safe manner.	2. Some of the equipment provided is being used appropriately, but there are many instances of inappropriate use.	3. Most of the equipment provided is being used appropriately, but there are a few instances of inappropriate use.	4. Almost all of the equipment provided is being used as intended and in a safe manner.	Note any inappropriate use of equipment (be specific) as well as any creative use of equipment (be specific).
(15) Physical Altercations: Volume AND intensity of any physical contact, including a threat of violence (raised fist). Don't judge intent of hitting.				
1. There were several physical altercations between students.	2. There were some physical altercations between students.	3. There were few physical altercations between students.	4. There were no physical altercation between students.	Describe pattern of physical altercations. Describe kids involved (gender, race, sport players, outcasts, etc.). Describe kids involved (gender, race, sport players, outcasts, etc.).

1	2	3	4	Notes

If **no**, skip the following question and **enter "n/a"** into scoring for the following indicator. If yes, answer the following question and enter the appropriate score.

(16) Adult Intervention—Physical Altercations:

1	2	3	4	Notes
1. Adults did not intervene between students after seeing physical altercations.	2. Adults intervened after seeing physical altercations but did so in a nonconstructive manner.	3. Adults intervened after seeing physical altercations and sometimes did so in a constructive manner.	4. Adults intervened after seeing physical altercations and almost always did so in a constructive way.	*Describe how adults handle physical altercations.*

(17) Student Communication: Absence of negative language or absence of positive language = neutral playground.

1	2	3	4	Notes
1. Hardly any communication (verbal or nonverbal) between students is positive and encouraging toward each other.	2. Very little communication (verbal or nonverbal) between students is positive and encouraging toward each other.	3. Most of the communication (verbal or nonverbal) between students is positive and encouraging toward each other.	4. Almost all of communication (verbal or nonverbal) between students is positive and encouraging toward each other.	*Describe the pattern of verbal altercations. Describe kids involved (gender, race, sport players, outcasts, etc.). Describe patterns of positive language. Describe kids involved (gender, race, sport players, outcasts, etc.).*

Did you observe students using negative verbal and nonverbal communication to each other **that was seen by supervising adults?** If **no**, skip the following question and **enter "n/a"** into scoring for the following indicator. If yes, answer the following question and enter the appropriate score.

(18) Adult Intervention—Negative Communication: Verbal AND nonverbal communication.

1	2	3	4
1. Adults did not intervene between students after seeing negative communication.	2. Adults intervened after seeing negative communication but did so in a nonconstructive manner.	3. Adults intervened after seeing negative communication and sometimes did so in a constructive manner.	4. Adults intervened after seeing negative communication and almost always did so in a constructive way.

(19) Student Disagreements—Rules: Score down when disagreement disrupts the flow of the game.

1	2	3	4	Notes
1. There were several disagreements about rules between students.	2. There were some disagreements about rules between students.	3. There were few disagreements about rules between students.	4. There were no disagreements about rules between students.	*What games have the most disagreements? How are students resolving their disagreements?*

(20) Conflict Resolution: Conflict resolution skills: negotiate, walk away, rock-paper-scissors.

1	2	3	4	Notes
1. Students demonstrate hardly any strategies for resolving conflicts on their own.	2. Students demonstrate a few strategies for resolving conflicts on their own, but a lot of adult support is needed.	3. Students demonstrate adequate strategies for resolving conflicts on their own, but some adult support is needed.	4. Students demonstrate strategies to resolve their conflict without adult intervention or there is no evident conflict.	*Describe conflict resolution strategies noted. Describe any demographic differences (e.g., gender, race, ability).*

Appendix 2

1	2	3	4	Notes
(21) Adult Behavior: Encourage students to participate, get students involved, don't put kids on wall or yell at them. Behavior doesn't have to be persistent during ENTIRE recess.				
1. Hardly any adults model positive culture (e.g., positive language, supporting conflict resolution skills).	2. A few adults model positive culture (e.g., positive language, supporting conflict resolution skills).	3. Many adults model positive culture (e.g., positive language, supporting conflict resolution skills).	4. Almost all adults model positive culture (e.g., positive language, supporting conflict resolution skills).	*Note adult participation. What are adults doing? Are there differences in what adults are doing (male versus female)? How are children responding to adults (hanging around them, asking them to play, etc.)? If adults play, who is playing what?*
(22) Adult Positioning: Over the course of recess, assess supervision coverage.				
1. Hardly any supervising adults are strategically positioned to view students in the recess play space (i.e., adults are huddled together).	2. Some of the supervising adults are strategically positioned to view students in the recess play space, but many students are unsupervised.	3. Many of the supervising adults are strategically positioned to view students in the recess play space, but some students are unsupervised.	4. Almost all of the supervising adults are strategically positioned to view students in the recess play space.	
(23) Adult Engagement: Adults are engaged in facilitating play (at some point).				
1. Hardly any adults are playing games or engaged with students.	2. A few adults are playing games and/or engaged with students.	3. Some adults are playing games and/or engaged with students.	4. Almost all adults are playing games and engaged with students.	
(24) Transition(s) from Recess: Consider time it takes to transition.				
1. Hardly any transitions to the classroom from recess are organized and smooth.	2. Some transitions to the classroom from recess are organized and smooth.	3. Most transitions to the classroom from recess are organized and smooth.	4. All transitions to the classroom from recess are organized and smooth.	*Note behaviors observed during transition to recess. Note any observed rules (e.g., what were monitors telling kids?).*

Other Notes:

What did they playground look like? Indicate where kids tend to congregate and where different games are.

Great Recess Framework Scoring Sheet

School:							Additional Notes:
Date:							
Rater:							
GRF Question	Recess 1	Recess 2	Recess 3	Recess 4	Recess 5	Recess 6	
	Grade(s): Start Time: End Time:	Grade(s): Start Time: End Time:	Grade(s): Start Time: End Time:	Grade(s): Start Time: End Time:	Grade(s): Start Time: End Time:	Grade(s): Start Time: End Time:	
1							
2							
3							
4							
5							
6							
7							
8							
9							
10							
11							
12							
13							
14							
15							
16							
17							
18							
19							
20							
21							
22							
23							
24							

NOTES

INTRODUCTION

1. All staff, school, and district names in the book are pseudonyms to preserve the confidentiality of respondents.
2. Amanda Conlin and Larissa Barbe, "Why and How You Should Take Breaks at Work," *Psychology Today Blog*, April 3, 2017, https://www.psychologytoday.com/us/blog/the-wide-wide-world-psychology/201704/why-and-how-you-should-take-breaks-work.
3. Susan Scutti, "Yes, Sitting Too Long Can Kill You, Even if You Exercise," *CNN*, September 12, 2017, https://www.cnn.com/2017/09/11/health/sitting-increases-risk-of-death-study/index.html.
4. Ben Dolnick, "Letter of Recommendation: Kitchen Timer," *New York Times*, November 24, 2015, https://www.nytimes.com/2015/11/29/magazine/letter-of-recommendation-kitchen-timer.html.
5. Center on Education Policy, *Instructional Time in Elementary Schools: A Closer Look at Changes for Specific Subjects* (Washington, DC: Center on Education Policy, 2008).
6. "United Nations Convention on the Rights of the Child," IPAworld, May 1, 2012, http://ipaworld.org/childs-right-to-play/uncrc-article-31/un-convention-on-the-rights-of-the-child-1/.
7. Cynthia L. Ogden, Margaret D. Carroll, Hannah G. Lawman, Cheryl D. Fryar, Deanna Kruszon-Moran, Brian K. Kit, and Katherine M. Flegal, "Trends in Obesity Prevalence Among Children and Adolescents in the United States, 1988–1994 Through 2013–2014," *JAMA* 315, no. 21 (2016): 2292–99.
8. Robert Murray and Catherine Ramstetter, "The Crucial Role of Recess in School," *Pediatrics* 131, no. 1 (2013): 183–88.
9. Centers for Disease Control and Prevention and SHAPE America—Society of Health and Physical Educators, *Strategies for Recess in Schools* (Atlanta, GA: Centers for Disease Control and Prevention, US Department of Health and Human Services, 2017); Centers for Disease Control and Prevention and SHAPE America—Society of Health and Physical Educators, *Recess Planning in Schools: A Guide to Putting Strategies for Recess into Practice* (Atlanta, GA: Centers for Disease Control and Prevention, US Department of Health and Human Services, 2017).

10. Rebecca A. London, Lisa Westrich, Katie Stokes-Guinan, and Milbrey McLaughlin, "Playing Fair: The Contribution of High-Functioning Recess to Overall School Climate in Low-Income Elementary Schools," *Journal of School Health* 85, no. 1 (2015): 53–60; Jane Fortson, Susanne James-Burdumy, Martha Bleeker, Nicholas Beyler, Rebecca A. London, Lisa Westrich, Katie Stokes-Guinan, and Sebastian Castrechini, *Impact and Implementation Findings from an Experimental Evaluation of Playworks: Effects on School Climate, Academic Learning, Student Social Skills and Behavior* (Princeton, NJ: Mathematica Policy Research, 2013).
11. Murray and Ramstetter, "Crucial Role of Recess," 183–88.
12. Maria C. Caterino and Emanuel D. Polak, "Effects of Two Types of Activity on the Performance of Second-, Third-, and Fourth-Grade Students on a Test of Concentration," *Perceptual and Motor Skills* 89, no. 1 (1999): 245–48; Stuart J. H. Biddle and Mavis Asare, "Physical Activity and Mental Health in Children and Adolescents: A Review of Reviews," *British Journal of Sports Medicine* 45, no. 11 (2011): 886–95.
13. John J. Ratey and Eric Hagerman, *Spark: The Revolutionary New Science of Exercise and the Brain* (New York: Little Brown & Company, 2008).
14. Catherine N. Rasberry, Sarah M. Lee, Leah Robin, B. A. Laris, Lisa A. Russell, Karin K. Coyle, and Allison J. Nihiser, "The Association Between School-Based Physical Activity, Including Physical Education, and Academic Performance: A Systematic Review of the Literature," *Preventive Medicine* 52 (2011): S10–S20.
15. Romina M. Barros, Ellen J. Silver, and Ruth E. K. Stein, "School Recess and Group Classroom Behavior," *Pediatrics* 123, no. 2 (2009): 431–36.
16. Fortson et al., *Impact and Implementation Findings*.
17. London et al., "Playing Fair," 53–60.
18. Regina M. Milteer, Kenneth R. Ginsburg, and Deborah Ann Mulligan, "The Importance of Play in Promoting Healthy Child Development and Maintaining Strong Parent-Child Bond: Focus on Children in Poverty," *Pediatrics* 129, no. 1 (2012): e204–e213; Sandra Waite-Stupiansky and Marcia Findlay, "The Fourth R: Recess and Its Link to Learning," *The Educational Forum* 66, no. 1 (2002): 16–25.
19. Collaborative for Academic, Social, and Emotional Learning, *Effective Social and Emotional Learning Programs—Preschool and Elementary School Edition* (Chicago, IL: CASEL, 2013).
20. Joseph A. Durlak, Roger P. Weissberg, Allison B. Dymnicki, Rebecca D. Taylor, and Kriston B. Schellinger, "The Impact of Enhancing Students' Social and Emotional Learning: A Meta-Analysis of School-Based Universal Interventions," *Child Development* 82, no. 1 (2011): 405–32; Joseph E. Zins and Maurice J. Elias, "Social and Emotional Learning: Promoting the Development of All Students," *Journal of Educational and Psychological Consultation* 17, no. 2–3 (2007): 233–55.
21. "School Climate," US Department of Education, National Center on Safe Supportive Learning Environments, https://safesupportivelearning.ed.gov/safe-and-healthy-students/school-climate.
22. Amrit Thapa, Jonathan Cohen, Shawn Guffey, and Ann Higgins-D'Alessandro, "A Review of School Climate Research," *Review of Educational Research* 83, no. 3 (2013): 357–85.
23. Sandy J. Slater, Lisa Nicholson, Jamie Chriqui, Lindsey Turner, and Frank Chaloupka, "The Impact of State Laws and District Policies on Physical Education and

Recess Practices in a Nationally Representative Sample of US Public Elementary Schools," *Archives of Pediatrics & Adolescent Medicine* 166, no. 4 (2012): 311–16.
24. Centers for Disease Control and Prevention, *Overview: School Health Policies and Programs Study 2000* (Atlanta, GA: Centers for Disease Control and Prevention, US Department of Health and Human Services, 2000); Centers for Disease Control and Prevention, *Results from the School Health Policies and Practices Study 2014* (Atlanta, GA: Centers for Disease Control and Prevention, US Department of Health and Human Services, 2015).
25. Centers for Disease Control and Prevention and Bridging the Gap Research Program, *Strategies for Supporting Recess in Elementary Schools, Update for the 2012–13 School Year* (Atlanta, GA: US Department of Health and Human Services, 2014).
26. Barros et al., "School Recess," 431–36.
27. Lindsey Turner, Jamie F. Chriqui, and Frank J. Chaloupka, "Withholding Recess from Elementary School Students: Policies Matter," *Journal of School Health* 83, no. 8 (2013): 533–41.

CHAPTER 1

1. Dirk Johnson, "Many Schools Putting an End to Child's Play," *New York Times*, April 7, 1998.
2. Carol Chmelynski, "Is Recess Needed?," *Education Digest* 64, no. 4 (1998): 67.
3. Debra Nussbaum, "Before Children Ask, 'What's Recess?,'" *New York Times*, December 10, 2006.
4. Amrit Thapa, Jonathan Cohen, Shawn Guffey, and Ann Higgins-D'Alessandro, "A Review of School Climate Research," *Review of Educational Research* 83, no. 3 (2013): 357–85.
5. Angela K. Dills, Hillary N. Morgan, and Kurt W. Rotthoff, "Recess, Physical Education, and Elementary School Student Outcomes," *Economics of Education Review* 30, no. 5 (2011): 889–900.
6. Percentage calculated using data provided on the Georgia Department of Education website: http://www.gadoe.org/Pages/Home.aspx.
7. Stuart Luppescu, Elaine M. Allensworth, Paul Moore, Marisa de la Torre, and James Murphy, *Trends in Chicago's Schools Across Three Eras of Reform* (Chicago, IL: Chicago Consortium on School Research, 2011).
8. "Kidscount," Annie E. Casey Foundation, https://datacenter.kidscount.org/topics.
9. Romina M. Barros, Ellen J. Silver, and Ruth E. K. Stein, "School Recess and Group Classroom Behavior," *Pediatrics* 123, no. 2 (2009): 431–36.
10. Low-income students are those with family incomes less than $25,000, and higher-income students have family incomes greater than $75,000.
11. Monika Stodolska, Juan Carlos Acevedo, and Kimberly J. Shinew, "Gangs of Chicago: Perceptions of Crime and Its Effect on the Recreation Behavior of Latino Residents in Urban Communities," *Leisure Sciences* 31, no. 5 (2009): 466–82.
12. Monika Stodolska, Kimberly J. Shinew, Juan Carlos Acevedo, and Caterina G. Roman, "'I Was Born in the Hood': Fear of Crime, Outdoor Recreation and Physical Activity Among Mexican-American Urban Adolescents," *Leisure Sciences* 35, no. 1 (2013): 1–15.

13. Lisa M. Powell, Sandy Slater, and Frank J. Chaloupka, "The Relationship Between Community Physical Activity Settings and Race, Ethnicity and Socioeconomic Status," *Evidence-Based Preventive Medicine* 1, no. 2 (2004): 135–44.
14. Paul A. Estabrooks, Rebecca E. Lee, and Nancy C. Gyurcsik, "Resources for Physical Activity Participation: Does Availability and Accessibility Differ by Neighborhood Socioeconomic Status?," *Annals of Behavioral Medicine* 25, no. 2 (2003): 100–104.
15. The National Physical Activity Plan, *The 2016 United States Report Card on Physical Activity for Children and Youth* (Columbia, SC: The National Physical Activity Plan, 2016).
16. Annette Lareau, *Unequal Childhoods: Class, Race, and Family Life* (Oakland, CA: University of California Press, 2011).
17. Tiffani Chin and Meredith Phillips, "Social Reproduction and Child-Rearing Practices: Social Class, Children's Agency, and the Summer Activity Gap," *Sociology of Education* 77, no. 3 (2004): 185–210.
18. Meenakshi Fernandes and Roland Sturm, "Facility Provision in Elementary Schools: Correlates with Physical Education, Recess, and Obesity," *Preventive Medicine* 50 (2010): S30–S35.
19. Nicholas Day, "The Rebirth of Recess: How Do You Introduce Recess to Kids Who Have Never Left the Classroom?," *Slate*, August 12, 2012.
20. Anthony D. Pellegrini, *Recess: Its Role in Education and Development* (Mahwah, NJ: Psychology Press, 2006), 37.
21. Rebecca A. London, Lisa Westrich, Katie Stokes-Guinan, and Milbrey McLaughlin, "Playing Fair: The Contribution of High-Functioning Recess to Overall School Climate in Low-Income Elementary Schools," *Journal of School Health* 85, no. 1 (2015): 53–60.
22. Amrit Thapa, Jonathan Cohen, Shawn Guffey, and Ann Higgins-D'Alessandro, "A Review of School Climate Research," *Review of Educational Research* 83, no. 3 (2013): 357–85.
23. Centers for Disease Control and Prevention, *Results from the School Health Policies and Practices Study 2014* (Atlanta, GA: Centers for Disease Control and Prevention, US Department of Health and Human Services, 2015).
24. Lindsey Turner, Jamie F. Chriqui, and Frank J. Chaloupka, "Withholding Recess from Elementary School Students: Policies Matter," *Journal of School Health* 83, no. 8 (2013): 533–41.
25. Julie C. Rusby, Ted K. Taylor, and E. Michael Foster, "A Descriptive Study of School Discipline Referrals in First Grade," *Psychology in the Schools* 44, no. 4 (2007): 333–50.
26. David Osher, Jane Coggshall, Greta Colombi, Darren Woodruff, Samantha Francois, and Trina Osher, "Building School and Teacher Capacity to Eliminate the School-to-Prison Pipeline," *Teacher Education and Special Education* 35, no. 4 (2012): 284–95.
27. Scott A. Spaulding, Larry K. Irvin, Robert H. Horner, Seth L. May, Monica Emeldi, Tary J. Tobin, and George Sugai, "Schoolwide Social-Behavioral Climate, Student Problem Behavior, and Related Administrative Decisions: Empirical Patterns from 1,510 Schools Nationwide," *Journal of Positive Behavior Interventions* 12, no. 2 (2010): 69–85.

28. US Government Accounting Office, *Discipline Disparities for Black Students, Boys, and Students with Disabilities* (Washington, DC: US Government Accounting Office, 2018).
29. Daniel J. Losen, Cheri L. Hodson, I. I. Keith, A. Michael, Katrina Morrison, and Shakti Belway, *Are We Closing the School Discipline Gap?* (Los Angeles, CA: University of California Los Angeles Center for Civil Rights Remedies, 2015).
30. Charles J. Russo and Carolyn Talbert-Johnson, "The Overrepresentation of African American Children in Special Education: The Resegregation of Educational Programming?," *Education and Urban Society* 29, no. 2 (1997): 136–48; Amanda L. Sullivan, "Disproportionality in Special Education Identification and Placement of English Language Learners," *Exceptional Children* 77, no. 3 (2011): 317–34.
31. Anthony D. Pellegrini, "The Recess Debate: A Disjuncture Between Educational Policy and Scientific Research," *American Journal of Play* 1, no. 2 (2008): 181–91.
32. Ron Schacter, "The End of Recess: Higher Standards Are Squeezing Out Playtime at Schools Throughout the Country," *District Administration* 41, no. 8 (2005): 36–41.
33. Vanessa McCray, "Atlanta Schools Change Recess Rules," *Atlanta Journal-Constitution*, November 14, 2017.
34. State of Georgia, http://www.legis.ga.gov/legislation/en-US/Display/20172018/HB/273.

CHAPTER 2
1. Gallup, *The State of Play: Gallup Survey of Principals on School Recess* (Princeton, NJ: Robert Wood Johnson Foundation, 2010).
2. The survey population included a mix of urban, suburban, and rural schools as well as those serving few, some, and many low socioeconomic status students. The largest single category of respondents was suburban principals serving schools with few students who received free and reduced price meals (23 percent). Because this book seeks to examine equity in recess provision, some of the charts in this chapter compare two groups of schools that combine the schools' geographic location and the students' socioeconomic levels: (1) urban low-income schools, which amount to a total of 11.6 percent of the respondents, or 225 schools; and (2) all others, which combines urban schools that serve higher socioeconomic status students as well as suburban and rural schools of all socioeconomic levels.
3. Where comparisons are made between urban low-income and other schools, differences are statistically significant.
4. Gallup, *The State of Play*.
5. In our day-long visits to each of the twelve schools, we observed a total of thirty-six different recess periods, with different mixtures of student age groups. Ten of the schools had one recess period per day at lunchtime, and two schools had two recess periods—one in the morning and one at lunchtime. Our observation reporting form asks observers to document the number of students sitting out, the reason (if it can be discerned), and whether they were boys or girls. I omit recesses that served students in middle school grades although we observed these in K–8 schools.
6. David Osher, George G. Bear, Jeffrey R. Sprague, and Walter Doyle, "How Can We Improve School Discipline?," *Educational Researcher* 39, no. 1 (2010): 48–58.

CHAPTER 3

1. Jessyka N. Larson, Timothy A. Brusseau, Benjamin Chase, Angela Heinemann, and James C. Hannon, "Youth Physical Activity and Enjoyment During Semi-Structured Versus Unstructured School Recess," *Open Journal of Preventive Medicine* 4, no. 8 (2014): 631; Brendon Hyndman, "Where to Next for School Playground Interventions to Encourage Active Play? An Exploration of Structured and Unstructured School Playground Strategies," *Journal of Occupational Therapy, Schools, & Early Intervention* 8, no. 1 (2015): 56–67.
2. Anita C. Bundy, Tim Luckett, Paul J. Tranter, Geraldine A. Naughton, Shirley R. Wyver, Jo Ragen, and Greta Spies, "The Risk Is That There Is 'No Risk': A Simple, Innovative Intervention to Increase Children's Activity Levels," *International Journal of Early Years Education* 17, no. 1 (2009): 33–45; Brendon Hyndman, Amanda C. Benson, Shahid Ullah, and Amanda Telford, "Evaluating the Effects of the Lunchtime Enjoyment Activity and Play (LEAP) School Playground Intervention on Children's Quality of Life, Enjoyment and Participation in Physical Activity," *BMC Public Health* 14, no. 1 (2014): 164.
3. Anna R. Beresin, "Play Counts: Pedometers and the Case for Recess," *International Journal of Play* 1, no. 2 (2012): 131–38.
4. Anthony D. Pellegrini, *Recess: Its Role in Education and Development* (Mahwah, NJ: Psychology Press, 2006).
5. Anna Beresin, *The Art of Play: Recess and the Practice of Invention* (Philadelphia, PA: Temple University Press, 2014).
6. Stefanie J. M. Verstraete, Greet M. Cardon, Dirk L. R. De Clercq, and Ilse M. M. De Bourdeaudhuij, "Increasing Children's Physical Activity Levels During Recess Periods in Elementary Schools: The Effects of Providing Game Equipment," *European Journal of Public Health* 16, no. 4 (2006): 415–19.
7. Nicola D. Ridgers, Gareth Stratton, Stuart J. Fairclough, and Jos W. R. Twisk, "Long-Term Effects of a Playground Markings and Physical Structures on Children's Recess Physical Activity Levels," *Preventive Medicine* 44, no. 5 (2007): 393–97.
8. Lisa J. Willenberg, Rosie Ashbolt, Dionne Holland, Lisa Gibbs, Colin MacDougall, Jan Garrard, Julie B. Green, and Elizabeth Waters, "Increasing School Playground Physical Activity: A Mixed Methods Study Combining Environmental Measures and Children's Perspectives," *Journal of Science and Medicine in Sport* 13, no. 2 (2010): 210–16.
9. Martha Bleeker, Nicholas Beyler, Susanne James-Burdumy, and Jane Fortson, "The Impact of Playworks on Boys' and Girls' Physical Activity During Recess," *Journal of School Health* 85, no. 3 (2015): 171–78; Susanne James-Burdumy, Nicholas Beyler, Kelley Borradaile, Martha Bleeker, Alyssa Maccarone, and Jane Fortson, "The Impact of Playworks on Students' Physical Activity by Race/Ethnicity: Findings from a Randomized Controlled Trial," *Journal of Physical Activity and Health* 13, no. 3 (2016): 275–80; William V. Massey, Megan B. Stellino, Megan Holliday, Travis Godbersen, Rachel Rodia, Greta Kucher, and Megan Wilkison, "The Impact of a Multi-Component Physical Activity Programme in Low-Income Elementary Schools," *Health Education Journal* 76, no. 5 (2017): 517–30.
10. For more information, see https://www.recesslab.org.
11. US Consumer Product Safety Commission, *Public Playground Safety Handbook* (Bethesda, MD: US Consumer Product Safety Commission, 2015).

12. See, for instance, the Playworks game archive at https://www.playworks.org/game-library/ or this archive of classic recess games at https://www.wired.com/2009/08/simpleoutdoorplay/.
13. For instance, see http://korkat.com/playground-grants/. Also, organizations like City Year help to build new playgrounds, and Peaceful Playgrounds creates school play yard blueprints. Both have resources available on their websites.

CHAPTER 4

1. Melinda Bossenmeyer, *Positive Alternatives to Withholding Recess* (Lake Elsinore, CA: Peaceful Playgrounds, 2013).
2. Center for Science in the Public Interest, *Alternative School Discipline Options to Withholding Recess* (Washington, DC: Center for Science in the Public Interest, 2016).
3. Playworks rules for these games can be found on their website. Three-line soccer rules are at https://www.playworks.org/game-library/three-lines-soccer/.
4. The game and alternative ways to play are described by Playworks at https://www.playworks.org/game-library/ro-sham-bo-or-rock-paper-scissors/.

CHAPTER 5

1. Maurice J. Elias, Joseph E. Zins, Roger P. Weissberg, Karin S. Frey, Mark T. Greenberg, Norris M. Haynes, Rachael Kessler, Mary E. Schwab-Stone, and Timothy P. Shriver, *Promoting Social and Emotional Learning: Guidelines for Educators* (Alexandria, VA: Association for Supervision and Curriculum Development, 1997).
2. Linda Dusenbury and Roger P. Weissberg, *Social Emotional Learning in Elementary School: Preparation for Success* (College Park, PA: Edna Bennett Pierce Prevention Research Center, Pennsylvania State University, 2017).
3. National Research Council, *Education for Life and Work: Developing Transferable Knowledge and Skills in the 21st Century* (Washington, DC: National Academies Press, 2013); Hugh Price, *Social and Emotional Development: The Next School Reform Frontier* (Washington, DC: Brookings Institution, 2015).
4. Elias et al., *Promoting Social and Emotional Learning*.
5. Kimberly A. Schonert-Reichl and Roger P. Weissberg, "Social and Emotional Learning: Children," in *Encyclopedia of Primary Prevention and Health Promotion*, ed. Thomas P. Gullotta and Martin Bloom (New York: Springer, 2014), 936–49.
6. Dusenbury and Weissberg, *Social Emotional Learning in Elementary School*.
7. Joseph A. Durlak, Roger P. Weissberg, Allison B. Dymnicki, Rebecca D. Taylor, and Kriston B. Schellinger, "The Impact of Enhancing Students' Social and Emotional Learning: A Meta-Analysis of School-Based Universal Interventions," *Child Development* 82, no. 1 (2011): 405–32.
8. Durlak et al., "Impact of Enhancing," 406.
9. Sara E. Rimm-Kaufman and Chris S. Hulleman, "Social and Emotional Learning in Elementary School Settings: Identifying Mechanisms That Matter," in *The Handbook of Social and Emotional Learning*, ed. Joseph A. Durlak, Celene E. Domitrovich, Roger P. Weissberg, and Thomas P. Gullotta (New York: Guilford Press, 2015), 151–66.
10. Elias et al., *Promoting Social and Emotional Learning*.

11. Rimm-Kaufman and Hulleman, "Social and Emotional Learning in Elementary School," 151–66.
12. Durlak et al., "Impact of Enhancing."
13. Jane Fortson, Susanne James-Burdumy, Martha Bleeker, Nicholas Beyler, Rebecca A. London, Lisa Westrich, Katie Stokes-Guinan, and Sebastian Castrechini, *Impact and Implementation Findings from an Experimental Evaluation of Playworks: Effects on School Climate, Academic Learning, Student Social Skills and Behavior* (Princeton, NJ: Mathematica Policy Research, 2013).
14. Sean Grant, Laura S. Hamilton, Stephani L. Wrabel, Celia J. Gomez, Anamarie Whitaker, Jennifer Tamargo, Fatih Unlu, Emilio R. Chavez-Herrerias, Garrett Baker, Mark Barrett, Mark Harris, and Alyssa Ramos, *Social and Emotional Learning Interventions* (Santa Monica, CA: RAND Corporation, 2017).
15. In total, twelve schools were assigned to the control condition and seventeen to the treatment condition. Data collections were completed in spring of the school year at all twenty-nine schools, and findings were compared between the treatment and control schools to establish the impact of Playworks.
16. Fortson et al., *Impact and Implementation Findings*.
17. Kristine A. Madsen, Katherine Hicks, and Hannah Thompson, "Physical Activity and Positive Youth Development: Impact of a School-Based Program," *Journal of School Health* 81, no. 8 (2011): 462–70.
18. Martha Bleeker, Nicholas Beyler, Susanne James-Burdumy, and Jane Fortson, "The Impact of Playworks on Boys' and Girls' Physical Activity During Recess," *Journal of School Health* 85, no. 3 (2015): 171–78.
19. Susanne James-Burdumy, Nicholas Beyler, Kelley Borradaile, Martha Bleeker, Alyssa Maccarone, and Jane Fortson, "The Impact of Playworks on Students' Physical Activity by Race/Ethnicity: Findings from a Randomized Controlled Trial," *Journal of Physical Activity and Health* 13, no. 3 (2016): 275–80.
20. Rebecca A. London and Kirsten Standeven, *Building a Culture of Health Through Safe and Healthy Elementary School Recess* (Princeton, NJ: Robert Wood Johnson Foundation, 2017).
21. Jacob Leos-Urbel and Monika Sanchez, *The Relationship Between Playworks Participation and Student Attendance in Two School Districts* (Stanford, CA: John W. Gardner Center for Youth and Their Communities, 2015).
22. Amrit Thapa, Jonathan Cohen, Shawn Guffey, and Ann Higgins-D'Alessandro, "A Review of School Climate Research," *Review of Educational Research* 83, no. 3 (2013): 357–85.
23. "What Is School Climate?," National School Climate Center, https://www.schoolclimate.org/about/our-approach/what-is-school-climate.
24. David Osher and Julia Berg, *School Climate and Social and Emotional Learning: The Integration of Two Approaches* (State College, PA: Edna Bennet Pierce Prevention Research Center, Pennsylvania State University, 2017).
25. Maurice J. Elias, Larry Leverett, Joan Cole Duffell, Neil Humphrey, Cesalie Stepney, and Joseph Ferrito, "Integrating SEL with Related Prevention and Youth Development Approaches," in *The Handbook of Social and Emotional Learning*, ed. Joseph A. Durlak, Celene E. Domitrovich, Roger P. Weissberg, and Thomas P. Gullotta (New York: Guilford Press, 2015), 33–49.

26. Rebecca A. London, Lisa Westrich, Katie Stokes-Guinan, and Milbrey McLaughlin, "Playing Fair: The Contribution of High-Functioning Recess to Overall School Climate in Low-Income Elementary Schools," *Journal of School Health* 85, no. 1 (2015): 53–60.

CHAPTER 6

1. J. Larry Brown and Ernesto Pollitt, "Malnutrition, Poverty and Intellectual Development," *Scientific American* 274, no. 2 (1996): 38–43; Katherine Alaimo, Christine M. Olson, and Edward A. Frongillo, "Food Insufficiency and American School-Aged Children's Cognitive, Academic, and Psychosocial Development," *Pediatrics* 108, no. 1 (2001): 44–53.
2. Kristen S. Slack and Joan Yoo, "Food Hardship and Child Behavior Problems Among Low-Income Children," *Social Service Review* 79, no. 3 (2005): 511–36; Diana F. Jyoti, Edward A. Frongillo, and Sonya J. Jones, "Food Insecurity Affects School Children's Academic Performance, Weight Gain, and Social Skills," *Journal of Nutrition* 135, no. 12 (2005): 2831–39.
3. Monica Hunsberger, Paul McGinnis, Jamie Smith, Beth Ann Beamer, and Jean O'Malley, "Elementary School Children's Recess Schedule and Dietary Intake at Lunch: A Community-Based Participatory Research Partnership Pilot Study," *BMC Public Health* 14, no. 1 (2014): 156; Ethan A. Bergman, Nancy S. Buergel, Timothy F. Englund, and Annaka Femrite, "The Relationship of Meal and Recess Schedules to Plate Waste in Elementary Schools," *Journal of Child Nutrition & Management* 28, no. 2 (2004): 1–10.
4. Tara Parker-Pope, "Play, then Eat: Shift May Bring Gains at School," *New York Times*, January 26, 2010.
5. Bergman et al., "The Relationship of Meal and Recess Schedules," 1–10.
6. "Timing and Duration Matters for School Lunch and Recess: Understanding the Relationship Between What Students Eat at Lunch and Physical Activity During Recess Could Inform Policies That Promote Healthy Behaviors," *Science Daily*, April 24, 2017.
7. Centers for Disease Control and Prevention, *Results from the School Health Policies and Practices Study 2016* (Atlanta, GA: Centers for Disease Control and Prevention, US Department of Health and Human Services, 2017).
8. Alice Jo Rainville, Kay N. Wolf, and Deborah H. Carr, "Recess Placement Prior to Lunch in Elementary Schools: What Are the Barriers," *Journal of Child Nutrition & Management* 30, no. 2 (2006): 1–10.
9. Timothy D. Walker, "How Finland Keeps Kids Focused Through Free Play," *The Atlantic*, June 30, 2014.
10. Henna L. Haapala, Mirja H. Hirvensalo, Kaarlo Laine, Lauri Laakso, Harto Hakonen, Anna Kankaanpää, Taru Lintunen, and Tuija H. Tammelin, "Recess Physical Activity and School-Related Social Factors in Finnish Primary and Lower Secondary Schools: Cross-Sectional Associations," *BMC Public Health* 14, no. 1 (2014): 1114.
11. Deborah Rhea and Michelle Bauml, "An Innovative Whole Child Approach to Learning: The LiiNK Project," *Childhood Education*, 94, no. 2 (2018): 56–63.
12. Centers for Disease Control and Prevention and SHAPE America—Society of Health and Physical Educators, *Recess Planning in Schools: A Guide to Putting*

Strategies for Recess into Practice (Atlanta, GA: Centers for Disease Control and Prevention, US Department of Health and Human Services, 2017).

13. Centers for Disease Control and Prevention and SHAPE America—Society of Health and Physical Educators, *Strategies for Recess in Schools* (Atlanta, GA: Centers for Disease Control and Prevention, US Department of Health and Human Services, 2017).

CHAPTER 7

1. Cheryl D. Fryar, Margaret D. Carroll, and Cynthia L. Ogden, *Prevalence of Overweight and Obesity Among Children and Adolescents: United States, 1963–1965 Through 2011–2012* (Washington, DC: National Center for Health Statistics, 2014).
2. Marion Burros, "A New Approach to Childhood Obesity Urged," *New York Times*, October 1, 2004.
3. Catherine Ramstetter and Robert Murray, "Time to Play: Recognizing the Benefits of Recess," *American Educator* 41, no. 1 (2017): 17.
4. "Local School Wellness Policies," https://www.fns.usda.gov/school-meals/local-school-wellness-policy.
5. Jamie Chriqui, Elissa Resnick, Linda Schneider, Rebecca Schermbeck, Tessa Adcock, Violeta Carrion, and Frank Chaloupka, *School District Wellness Policies: Evaluating Progress and Potential for Improving Children's Health Five Years After the Federal Mandate* (Princeton, NJ: Robert Wood Johnson Foundation, 2013).
6. Susan P. Harvey, Deborah Markenson, and Cheryl A. Gibson, "Assessing School Wellness Policies and Identifying Priorities for Action: Results of a Bi-State Evaluation," *Journal of School Health* 88, no. 5 (2018): 359–69; Melissa J. Cox, Susan T. Ennett, Christopher L. Ringwalt, Sean M. Hanley, and James M. Bowling, "Strength and Comprehensiveness of School Wellness Policies in Southeastern US School Districts," *Journal of School Health* 86, no. 9 (2016): 631–37.
7. Elizabeth Piekarz, Rebecca Schermbeck, Sabrina Young, Julien Leider, Margaret Ziemann, and Jamie Chriqui, *School District Wellness Policies: Evaluating Progress and Potential for Improving Children's Health Eight Years After the Federal Mandate. School Years 2006–07 through 2013–14* (Chicago, IL: Bridging the Gap Program and the National Wellness Policy Study, Institute for Health Research and Policy, University of Illinois at Chicago, 2016).
8. The National Physical Activity Plan, *The 2016 United States Report Card on Physical Activity for Children and Youth* (Columbia, SC: The National Physical Activity Plan, 2016).
9. Centers for Disease Control and Prevention and SHAPE America—Society of Health and Physical Educators, *Strategies for Recess in Schools* (Atlanta, GA: Centers for Disease Control and Prevention, US Department of Health and Human Services, 2017).
10. These brief reports are available at https://www.shapeamerica.org/advocacy/advocacyresources_state.aspx.
11. Florida Department of Education, Memorandum, July 14, 2017, https://info.fldoe.org/docushare/dsweb/Get/Document-7967/dps-2017-85.pdf.
12. Ricardo Cano, "Two Recess Periods a Day Will Be Mandatory for Arizona's Younger Students Next School Year," *The Republic*, April 5, 2018.
13. State of New Jersey, https://www.njleg.state.nj.us/2018/Bills/S1000/847_R3.pdf.

14. State of Rhode Island, Recess Law, Chapter 157, H 7644: 16-22-4.2, June 27, 2016, http://www.rihsc.org/uploads/8/2/7/6/82768452/recess_law_handout.pdf.
15. Terri Peters, "The Right to Play: New Rhode Island Law Requires Recess in Elementary Schools," *TODAY*, July 26, 2016.
16. More Recess for Virginians, "Understanding the Recess Bill," https://morerecessforvirginians.org/wp-content/uploads/2018/04/VA-Recess-Bill-Explanation.pdf.
17. Nancy Stephens, "What's New for Fairview School Recess?," *USA Today Network*, July 25, 2017, https://www.tennessean.com/story/news/2017/07/25/whats-new-fairview-recess/509833001.
18. Centers for Disease Control and Prevention, *Results from the School Health Policies and Practices Study 2016* (Atlanta, GA: Centers for Disease Control and Prevention, US Department of Health and Human Services, 2017).
19. Office for Civil Rights, US Department of Education, "2017–18 Civil Rights Data Collection: List of CRDC Data Elements for School Year 2017–18," https://www2.ed.gov/about/offices/list/ocr/docs/2017-18-crdc-data-elements.pdf.
20. Centers for Disease Control and Prevention and SHAPE America—Society of Health and Physical Educators, *Strategies for Recess in Schools* (Atlanta, GA: Centers for Disease Control and Prevention, US Department of Health and Human Services, 2017).

CHAPTER 8

1. The Great Recess Framework is available at https://www.greatrecessframework.org; US Consumer Product Safety Commission, *Public Playground Safety Handbook* (Bethesda, MD: US Consumer Product Safety Commission, 2015).
2. For instance, see http://korkat.com/playground-grants/. Also, organizations like City Year help to build new playgrounds, and Peaceful Playgrounds creates school play yard blueprints. Both have resources available on their websites.

APPENDIX 2

1. William V. Massey, Megan B. Stellino, Sean P. Mullen, Jennette Claassen, and Megan Wilkison, "Development of the Great Recess Framework–Observational Tool to Measure Contextual and Behavioral Components of Elementary School Recess," *BMC Public Health* 18, no. 1 (2018): 394. For more information and training videos, visit https://www.greatrecessframework.org.

ACKNOWLEDGMENTS

This book is the culmination of many years of research and collaboration. I am truly grateful to my colleagues at Playworks, especially Jill Vialet, Elizabeth Cushing, and Jennette Claassen, from whom I have learned so much. They have been eager collaborators, patient teachers, and receptive learners as we have together created a generative research-practice partnership. Their passion for recess and knowledge of the field have worn off on me personally and professionally, and they make this work fun. This partnership and the research presented in this book were supported by generous funding from the Robert Wood Johnson Foundation.

I am extremely appreciative of my colleagues at the John W. Gardner Center for Youth and Their Communities at Stanford University and the University of California, Santa Cruz, with whom I worked closely on recess research projects. Together we collected data at schools across the country, stood at recess in the rain and the hot sun, laughed about how funny kids are, and shared somber stories of what we observed. Thank you especially to Lisa Westrich, Katie Stokes-Guinan, Nora Mallonee, Monika Sanchez, and Sebastian Castrechini, who worked tirelessly to help conceive of and revise our frameworks and findings until they were just right. I am especially indebted to Milbrey McLaughlin, who saw a partnership with Playworks as an opportunity too good to turn down. She was right.

Writing a book can be a lonely business, and I am grateful to my writing support team of Sharon Greene and Deborah Siegel. They read chapter drafts, offered sage advice, asked thought-provoking questions, shared my enthusiasm for all things recess, and cheered me on to the end. Thank you also to Wilson Sherman, whose graphic design expertise came at just the right moment.

Thank you to my family and friends, who encouraged me throughout the writing process and managed to convince me that they care about recess as much as I do. My husband, Rob, and my daughters, Zoe and Jessica, provide me with inspiration and hope. My parents, Sheila and Len, and my sister, Jen, expressed their ongoing support through their love and curiosity. I am grateful to my wonderful friends, who checked in with me about my progress and discussed the findings over shared meals, while hiking, at book club meetings, and on the high school softball bleachers.

Many children, teachers, principals, recess staff members, recess coaches, and Playworks professionals contributed to this research with their insights. These busy people took the time to sit and talk about recess, openly and thoughtfully, and I strove to represent their views accurately in the book. Although they are unnamed to preserve their confidentiality, these are the heroes of this story, and without their generosity and perspectives, this book would not have been possible.

ABOUT THE AUTHOR

REBECCA A. LONDON is a faculty member in the Sociology Department at the University of California, Santa Cruz. Her research focuses on understanding the challenges faced by disadvantaged children and youth and the ways that communities and community organizations support young people to be healthy and successful. She advocates for and utilizes a university-community partnership approach to elevate the relevance of university scholarship through alignment with the pressing challenges and realities faced by community agencies and organizations. Her work focuses on both policy and practice, and uses qualitative and quantitative methods. She has conducted research in multiple fields, including K–12 and postsecondary education, cross-sector approaches to "whole student" development, health and wellness, afterschool programs, and social welfare programs.

She is coeditor of *From Data to Action: A Community Approach to Improving Youth Outcomes* (with Milbrey McLaughlin, 2013). Her recent work has been published in scholarly journals such as the *Journal of School Health*, *Educational Researcher*, *Education Policy Analysis Archives*, and the *American Journal of Preventive Medicine*. Her research has also been featured by organizations that reach important policy audiences, including the Center for American Progress, the Robert Wood Johnson Foundation, and the Public Policy Institute of California, where she is a fellow in K–12 policy.

She views the policies and contexts that shape the lives of children and youth through an equity lens, promoting practices and solutions that support positive development and outcomes. She was the founding faculty director of the Student Success Evaluation and Research Center at the University of California, Santa Cruz, and is committed to fostering cultural inclusivity and equity in her own teaching practice.

INDEX

academic achievement, 7, 15, 39, 103
accountability, 3–4, 15–17, 153–154, 180
activity zones, 72, 175
administrators. *See* principals; school administrators
adult-peer relationships, 68
adult role models, 93–96
adult supervision, 29, 30, 36, 43, 52–56, 89, 95–96, 122–123
  See also recess monitors
adult workers, breaks for, 3
African American students, 17, 18, 28, 111, 178
American Academy of Pediatrics, 5, 7, 23, 64, 172, 180
Arizona, 163, 164
Arkansas, 160
Atlanta Public Schools, 8, 15–16, 17, 32
autism, 28

Baltimore, 8
basketball, 89–90
behavioral development, 83
behavioral expectations, 27
behavior issues, 9, 44–53, 86, 115–116, 122
bell schedule, 87, 134–143
Beresin, Anna, 65, 66
boys, disciplinary actions and, 28

breaks, 3, 16, 137
bullying, 5, 29, 36, 48, 92–93, 118–119, 122, 128, 173, 181

cafeteria space, for indoor recess, 99–100
California, 168
Canada, Benjamin O., 15, 17
Centers for Disease Control and Prevention, 5, 19, 26, 138, 151, 154, 158–159, 169, 172
challenges, 5, 100–102, 173
change, resistance to, 100–102
character development, 83, 102–103
Chicago Public Schools, 8, 18, 23
childhood obesity, 4, 7, 153
Child Nutrition and Special Supplemental Nutrition Program for Women, Infants, and Children Reauthorization Act, 155
choice, 173
Civil Rights Data Collection, 28
class game time, 102
classroom behavior, 7, 9
  See also behavior issues
classroom management, 86
coaches, 94, 95
code switching, 116
cognition, 7, 16, 24

Collaborative for Academic, Social, and Emotional Learning (CASEL), 107–108
Colorado, 160
Common Core State Standards, 32
compassion, 93
competition, 88, 89–90
"concerted cultivation," 22
conflict resolution, 29, 41, 48–49, 68, 81, 83, 91–93, 109, 118–122, 176–177
crime, 20
culture
    changing, 82
    organizational, 82
    of play, 63, 71, 72, 81–103, 175
    recess, 5, 25, 29–30, 61, 63, 72, 89, 117, 126, 162
    school, 15–16, 81, 102–103, 176
    of winning, 88–89

data collection, 165–167, 178–179
data gap, 19–20
decision-making skills, 108
depression, 7
disciplinary actions, 6, 17, 26–30, 32–33, 36, 44–53, 84–86, 161–163
disciplinary referrals, 5, 11, 27–28, 44, 48, 58, 85, 91, 122, 140, 172, 181
drugs, 20

Early Childhood Longitudinal Survey, 20
educational institutions, 4
    See also schools
education policy, 16–17, 32–33, 153–170
education reforms, 3–4, 7–8, 107, 146
elementary schools. *See* schools
emotional development
    adults and, 122–124
    conflict resolution and, 118–122
    focus on, 106–107
    key skills, 108

play and, 23–25
recess and, 7, 8, 12, 16, 32–33, 48–49, 64, 96, 105–129, 179–180
school climate and, 125–129
strategies for, 108–109
empathy, 7
English language learners, 17, 28, 105–106
English scores, 3–4, 16
equipment
    availability of, 31, 40, 62, 64, 67, 125, 142
    checkout of, 69, 72, 74, 175
    fixed, 31, 67
    lack of, 17
    loose, 31, 71–72, 78–79, 175
    updating, 175
    use of, 42
equity issues, 15–33
exercise. *See* physical activity
extracurricular activities, 22
extracurricular sports, 21–22

families, 73
federal policies, 154–159, 167–170
fighting, 48, 49–50, 77
Finland, 137
fixed equipment, 31, 67
Florida, 163–164
free and reduced-price lunch and breakfast programs, 18, 26, 37, 155, 168
free play, 6, 75, 164, 165, 173

Gallup, 37, 38, 39, 56, 138
games
    adult involvement in, 43–44, 57, 93–96, 100–101
    competitive, 89–90
    conflict resolution strategies for, 91–93
    inclusion in, 89–91
    learning, 102

in organized recess, 61–63, 67, 69–72, 74–79, 82–84
rules for, 75–78, 173
spaces for, 30, 31, 41, 72, 125

handwashing, 136
Healthy, Hunger-Free Kids Act, 155
high-income families, extracurricular activities and, 22
hunger, 135, 136
hygiene, 136

implicit learning, 108–109
inclusion, 83, 88–91, 121, 177
indoor recess, 98–100
institutional contexts, 41, 62–63, 65–66, 179
international students, performance comparisons with, 3
Iowa, 160

junior coaches, 96–97, 106, 113–115, 128, 145

Koplan, Jeffrey, 153

Latinx students, 18, 111
leadership opportunities, 81, 96–98, 113–115, 177
learning
  classroom, 16, 26, 134–135, 139
  conflict resolution strategies, 48–49, 91
  implicit, 108–109
  social and emotional, 23–25, 32, 44, 68, 100, 103, 105–129, 137–138, 156–159, 167
life lessons, 24–25, 29
LiiNK Project, 138

lining up, 86–87, 88
Little League baseball, 21
local school wellness policies, 155–157, 166, 168
low-income students
  access to outside space and, 20–21
  access to recess for, 38–39, 172
  elimination of recess from, 17, 18
  recess reforms and, 105–106
  restrictive recess policies and, 8–9, 23, 26, 38, 137, 159
lunch breaks, 3
lunch schedule, 134–137

Mathematica Policy Research, 10
math scores, 3–4, 16
minority students, 8–9, 16–19, 172
moderate to vigorous physical activity (MVPA), 64, 67
multiage recess, 139–141

National Academies' Institute of Medicine, 153, 155
National Center on Safe Supportive Learning Environments, 106
neighborhood safety, 20, 31, 35–36
New Jersey, 163
No Child Left Behind Act, 3, 4
nonfixed equipment, 31, 71–72, 78–79, 175
nutrition, 135

obesity rates, 4, 7, 64, 153
Office for Civil Rights, 167, 178
opportunity gap, 18–19
Oregon, 27
organizational culture, 82
organized recess, 6–7, 61–80, 164, 181
  impact of, 81–83
  philosophy of, 62, 66–67
  reactions to, 74–79

organized recess, *continued*
  research on, 66–68
  role of, 173–177
  roll out of, 72–74
  school context and, 62–63
  social and emotional learning and, 110–111
  steps to, 68–74, 174–176
organized sports, 21–22
outdoor space
  See also play yard space
  access to, 20–21

paraprofessionals, 47, 53, 79–80, 88, 126, 146, 149–151
partnerships
  with outside organizations, 95
  school district, 145–147
Peaceful Playgrounds, 151
peer relationships, 7, 81
Pellegrini, Anthony, 23–24, 25, 29, 65
physical activity
  benefits of, 7
  delinking discipline and, 161–163
  guidelines for, 64, 147, 158–159
  opportunities for, 4–5, 19, 20–21, 23, 43–44
  organized recess and, 67–68, 111
  recess and, 154, 155–156, 157, 169, 179
  requirements for, 160–161
physical education, 6, 15, 32, 43, 64, 70, 79, 98, 99, 102, 111, 139, 160
physical health, 64, 65
play
  culture of, 63, 71, 72, 81–103, 175
  free, 6, 75, 164, 165, 173
  importance of, 6, 23–24
  obstacles to, 20–23
  right to, 3–5, 171–183
  rough-and-tumble, 51
  social and emotional learning and, 23–25
  structured, 6, 75

  unstructured, 65–66
play fighting, 51
Playworks, 9–11, 37, 66–70, 74, 86, 92, 96, 99, 110–118, 122–128, 143–146, 148, 151
play yard space
  activity zones in, 72, 175
  amount of, 30–31
  assessment of, 70, 174
  equipment for. *see* equipment
  lack of, 17, 23
  organization of, 68–70, 73, 81
  updates to, 71, 175
  variety of, 62–63
policy considerations, 2–5, 174
  documentation improvement, 165–167
  limitations of existing policies, 167–170
  local, 133–152
  policy assessment, 70–71
  state and federal, 153–170
Positive Behavioral Intervention and Supports, 102
positive role models, 93–96
Presidential Youth Fitness Program, 158
President's Council on Sports, Fitness and Nutrition, 158
principals
  recess and, 37–39, 56–58, 75, 120–124, 144, 148, 172
  scheduling decisions by, 134–143
private schools, 168
productivity, 3, 4
public health crisis, 4–5
punishment
  alternative, 85
  withholding recess as, 3, 9, 17, 26–30, 32–33, 36, 37, 44–48, 57–58, 84–86, 161–163, 171–172

recess
  across the country, 35–58
  adult participation in, 43–44, 57, 93–96, 100–101

Index

adult supervision during, 52–56, 86–87, 93–97, 100–101, 122–123, 172
as afterthought, 2
behavior and discipline issues at, 28, 29, 44–53, 48–53
benefits of, 7, 16, 45, 154, 171
case for, 1–12
challenges with, 5, 100–102, 173
champions, 79–80, 143, 144–145, 147, 173–174
combining grades and classes at, 139–141
conflict resolution strategies for, 91–93, 118–122, 176–177
culture of play at, 63, 71, 72, 81–103, 175
current state of, 8–9, 16–17
customizing, 61–63
data gap, 19–20
definition of, 3
design of, 2, 5, 24, 29–30, 33
documentation of, 165–167
funding, 100
future of, 177–180
goals of, 64
guidelines for, 158–159
importance of, 5–8, 32–33, 61
improvements in, 43–44, 56–58, 111–118
inclusion during, 83, 88–91, 121, 177
indoor, 98–100
inequities in, 15–33, 38–39
lunch and, 134–137
mindset shift toward, 180–182
opportunity gap, 18–19
organized, 6–7, 61–82, 110–111, 164, 173–177, 181
overlapping periods for, 141–143
planning, 63, 66, 80
policy considerations, 2–5, 70–71, 133–152, 153–170, 174
principals and, 37–39, 56–58, 75, 120–124, 144, 148, 172
reduction and elimination of, 3–4, 15–16, 18, 25, 171–172
requiring, 84–86, 160–161, 163–165, 168
research on, 9–12, 37–38, 179–180
right to, 171–183
rules for, 78
scheduling of, 38–39, 84, 133–143
school contexts and, 62–63, 65–66
school value alignment with, 102–103
social and emotional learning and, 7, 8, 12, 16, 32–33, 48–49, 64, 96, 105–129, 179–180
staffing, 143–152
structured, 62, 63–66, 67, 173
student activities during, 40–42
student engagement at, 39–44, 88–91, 173
student leadership at, 81, 96–98, 113–115, 177
support for, 4, 5
time for, 38–39, 137–139
transitions to/from, 86–88, 110–111, 119–120
unregulated time for, 6
unstructured, 63–66
vision for, 182–183
withholding as punishment, 3, 9, 17, 26–30, 32–33, 36, 37, 44–48, 57–58, 84–86, 161–163, 171–172
"recess checkup" system, 70
recess coaches, 143–144, 147–150, 150–151, 176
recess culture, 5, 25, 29–30, 61, 63, 72, 89, 117, 126, 162
recess monitors, 45, 48, 53–56, 86–87, 93–96, 100–101, 117, 122–123, 169, 172
recreation spaces
See also play yard space
access to, 20–21
relationship building, 7
relationship skills, 108
resilience, 116
respect, 7
responsible decision-making, 108
restorative justice, 178

Rhode Island, 164, 165
Robert Wood Johnson Foundation, 10, 11, 37, 38, 39, 56, 138
rock-paper-scissors, 83, 89, 92, 120, 176
role models, 93–96
roughhousing, 51

school administrators
　organized recess and, 74–79
　recess and, 37–38, 120–122, 124, 143
　resistance to change and, 101
　scheduling decisions by, 134–143
　staff changes and, 145–146
school climate, 7–8, 16, 25, 44, 52, 81, 91, 97, 100, 110, 125–129, 154
school contexts, 41, 62–63, 65–66, 179
school culture, 15–16, 81, 102–103, 176
school discipline policies, 84–86
school district partnerships, 145–147
School Health Policies and Practices Study (SHPPS), 19, 26, 166–167
school nurse, 144–145
schools
　private, 168
　reduction/elimination of recess from, 3–4, 15–16, 18, 25, 171–172
　as safe havens, 36
　without playgrounds, 23
school-to-prison pipeline, 9, 27
school wellness policies, 155–157, 166, 168
self-awareness, 108
self-management, 108
self-perceptions, 27
self-regulation, 64, 136, 162
SHAPE America, 5, 138, 151, 154, 158–160, 169
sitting, breaks from, 3
soccer, 89–90
social and emotional learning (SEL), 23–25, 32, 44, 68, 100, 103, 105–129, 137–138, 156–159

social awareness, 108
social development
　adults and, 122–124
　conflict resolution and, 118–122
　focus on, 106–107
　key skills, 108
　play and, 23–25
　recess and, 7, 8, 32, 48–49, 64, 96, 105–129, 179–180
　school climate and, 125–129
　strategies for, 108–109
socialization, 27
social skills, 16
socioeconomic status, 22
South Carolina, 160
special education students, 17, 28
sports leagues, 21–22
standardized testing, 3–4, 16, 179
standards-based accountability, 3–4, 15, 16–17, 153–154, 180
state policies, 159–165, 167–170
structured play, 6, 75
structured recess, 62, 63–66, 67, 173
student achievement, 3–4, 39, 103
student government, 97–98
students
　adult interaction with, 43–44, 53–56, 57, 93–96, 100–102
　African American, 17, 18, 28, 111, 178
　behavior issues, 9, 48–53, 86, 115–116, 122
　engagement at recess by, 39–44, 88–91, 173
　international, 3
　Latinx, 18, 111
　leadership by, 81, 96–98, 113–115, 177
　lining up by, 86–87, 88
　minority, 8–9, 16–19, 172
　organized recess and, 73–79
　safety of, 95
　urban, 17
　white, 18–19
student-to-adult engagement, 81, 122–123

tag game, 41, 51
teachers
  organized recess and, 7, 73, 74–79
  as recess monitors, 53, 95
  recess transformation and, 101–102
  resistance to change and, 100–101
  withholding recess by, 9, 26, 32, 45, 48, 58
TeamUp, 111–114, 118, 120, 122, 126–128, 143, 149
teasing, 48
Tennessee, 164
tetherball, 90
three-line soccer, 89, 90
time management, 3
Title I funds, 100
transitions, 86–88, 110–111, 119–120

underfunded schools, 17
underperforming schools, 3–4, 17
United Nations Convention on the Rights of the Child, 4, 172

unstructured recess, 63–66
urban parks, 20
urban schools
  neighborhood safety and, 35–36
  play yard space at, 17, 30–31
  recess in, 38–39
urban students, 17
US Department of Education, 28, 39, 106, 155, 158, 167, 178
U.S. Report Card on Physical Activity for Children and Youth, 21, 158

vice principals, 144
Virginia, 164
weather, 30–31, 98, 99
wellness policies, 155–157, 166, 168
white students, 18–19
whole child, 180
winning, culture of, 88–89